P9-BTX-967

Also by WILLIAM PFAFF
(with EDMUND STILLMAN)

POWER AND IMPOTENCE
THE NEW POLITICS
THE POLITICS OF HYSTERIA

CONDEMNED
TO FREEDOM

CONDEMNED
TO FREEDOM

WILLIAM PFAFF

RANDOM HOUSE

New York

CARNEGIE LIBRARY
LIVINGSTONE COLLEGE
SALISBURY, N. C. 28144

Copyright © 1971 by William Pfaff

All rights reserved under International
and Pan-American Copyright Conventions.
Published in the United States
by Random House, Inc., New York,
and simultaneously in Canada
by Random House of Canada Limited, Toronto.

ISBN: 0-394-46923-2
Library of Congress Catalog Card Number: 70-143995

Manufactured in the United States of America
by The Colonial Press, Inc., Clinton, Massachusetts

2 4 6 8 9 7 5 3

First Edition

320.51
P523

85971

To N I C K and A L I X,
and to C A R O L Y N

ACKNOWLEDGMENTS

This is a Hudson Institute Book. I am grateful to my colleagues at the Institute, and especially to Herman Kahn, its director, and Max Singer, its president, and to the Institute's contractors, for their sympathetic support of this undertaking.

Many of these arguments were first made in a series of papers prepared for a discussion group of the Council on Foreign Relations which met during the winter of 1969–1970. I thank my associates in that group for their comments, and particularly Fritz Stern, its chairman, and William J. Barnds and David MacEachron of the Council staff.

To Anne Marsek, my particular gratitude.

Chapter IV appeared originally in *The New Yorker*, in somewhat different form.

CONTENTS

WILLIAM PFAFF

CHAPTER I

The Crisis
of Liberalism

L I B E R A L (adj, hence n *Liberal*; hence also *Liberalism* . . .).

1. L *līber*, free — whence prob *Līber*, the Roman god of growth — is akin to the syn Gr *eleutheros*, perh also to the OGmc words for 'people', as, e.g., OE *lēod*, OFris *liōd*, OS *liud*, OHG *liuti*, MHG *liute*, G *Leute*, esp if these words orig meant 'free people' as opp slaves . . .

— Eric Partridge, *Origins*

In the face of mass disintegration, however, one is bound to ask whether liberalism still is pertinent to our foremost social problems. To be free is to be separate and individual; thus liberalism has expressed and encouraged personal distinctness and individual activity as opposed to social coherence. Religious freedom has tended to mean purely personal belief; economic freedom, individual entrepreneurial activity; and intellectual freedom, solitary mental labor. It is true that both in principle and in historical fact liberalism has stood for voluntary association as well as for individualism. But its central theme has certainly been the single individual, and its attack on medieval social order could not be halted before a rather thorough atomization had been achieved. In short, liberalism has been a force making for disintegration. What can it mean now to men suffering from the dissolution of their contacts with nature, place, possessions, and their fellow men? The aspiration which arises from mass disintegration seems to run directly against the current of liberalism.

— Glenn Tinder

I

THE BLOOD is real; the abstract errors and follies of politics become monstrous actions. The crisis of liberalism begins in the political intellect, is translated by action, and people are bloodied in the result. Captain Ahab: "All my means are sane: my motives and object mad."

Mad because cut loose from real things and possibilities. The liberal governments of the West today are forfeiting the confidence of their publics. Marginal movements of avowed revolution have sprung into existence; but more important is that a much larger body of the middle classes and workers are uneasily estranged from liberal culture, and specifically from a liberal political culture which no longer seems able to provide justice — from liberal governments no longer able to convince the public of their willingness and competence to do justice.

The new radical movements on the Western left with their assault on liberal institutions have so absorbed our attention that we fail to notice how serious the general loss of political confidence has become. What comfortingly has been interpreted as a struggle over definable issues between the radical left and a conservative or centrist majority conceals the fact that the majority is alienated too. Its defense of "the system" is a function of its anger at the style and nihilism of the rebels, not an affirmation of confidence. The "hardhat" workers of America, the provincial bourgeoisies of Europe, are at the same time neo-

3

populist and *Poujadist* critics of that same liberal system. They were hostile to the "liberal establishment" before the young people knew there was such a thing. It is their children who man the line infantry regiments in the wars of liberal governments. They are the ones most critically affected by economic crisis. They have rebelled before against incompetent, irresponsible or unresponsive rule: in Europe in the 1920's and 1930's, when another generation of liberal governments failed. Their commitments today are contingent ones.

One radical argument about our situation holds that crisis arises from liberal society's discovery of its own absurdity. The liberal bourgeoisie experiences a crisis of conscience; it confronts, for the first time, the cruelty, folly and waste of liberal society. But the explanation is sentimental. Fifty years of polemics, and the self-conscious experience of modern political history, have forced home to the bourgeois liberal intelligentsia that action is "absurd," paradoxical in its effects, and that man alone too often is vile. "History has many cunning passages, contrived corridors/And issues, deceives with whispering ambitions,/Guides us by vanities . . . Neither fear nor courage saves us. Unnatural vices/Are fathered by our heroism. Virtues/Are forced upon us by our impudent crimes." Thus T. S. Eliot in 1920. Bourgeois society, like bourgeois poets, between the two wars celebrated its own and historical absurdity to the exclusion of nearly all else.*

The ahistorical complacence of European liberal society rushing into war in 1914 is wholly unrecapturable. It was only with the greatest difficulty that Hitler compelled the democracies to go to war again in 1939, to place any

---

* A section of source references begins on p. 197.

confidence again in the ability of violence to create, in the necessary phrase, a better world. Since then, except in America, fairly little has been expected from politics. To tell the bourgeois European veteran of depression, inflation, war and Resistance, that liberal society generates waste and violence is no news at all. His commitment to liberal society is more subtle — or inevitable — than that.

Still, it is a qualified commitment. There would be no upheaval of political confidence either in the West European nations or in the United States if only the young — contemptuous of history — were involved, or the young in support of a marginal radical intelligentsia. Those who speak only of the rebellion of students and the young are attempting to define away a movement which clearly is far bigger in its range of associations and implications. Those who go on to dismiss the students as merely acting out a furious revenge upon their fathers for having made their lives comfortable, practice a reductionist fantasy. The competence and moral authority of liberal government have come to be doubted by more than the young. And more than liberal government is in doubt: critical elements in the political culture which makes that kind of government possible have been brought into question. It is this which makes the present situation so serious.

In our politics the world "crisis" has been banged and blunted out of all precision. In this century the West has more often been in crisis than out of it. The European nations and the United States have been torn by crises of world war, colonial war, economic collapse, party struggle, despotic government and genocide. Since 1900 Germany has experienced Hohenzollern monarchy, socialist revolution, Weimar liberalism, the Third Reich, defeat, partition and a federal republic. France began this century as the Third Republic; it is now the Fifth. In Italy, Belgium, Spain, Portugal, Austria, Poland, liberal governments have been shaken or broken by linguistic or regional nationalism, ideological civil wars, revolutionary and reactionary movements of national "renaissance." The United States ended the nineteenth century in a furious domestic controversy over its war on Spain and seizure of Spain's Cuban and Philippine colonies. It began this century intervening in China to put down the Boxer Rebellion, intervening in the Dominican Republic to collect debts, disputing with Japan over Americans' racist treatment of Japanese schoolchildren in California — and with the assassination, by an anarchist, of President McKinley. Yet, despite two world wars, a cold war and the Great Depression, liberal government in this country was never seriously threatened. Possibly our present anxiety is overwrought?

The answer begins with the evidence we have in the United States (to speak only of this country for the moment) of political unrest among the urban poor and the black and Spanish-speaking minorities, complex student unrest, a disquieted and increasingly resentful lower middle class of small property owners, tradesmen and skilled workers, themselves only recently escaped from poverty and the slums, the re-emergence of a radical left-wing intelligentsia and of avowedly revolutionary movements. There is a new affinity among a minority for theories justifying political violence, and a mounting practice of violence: political assassinations, political murders, bombings, "trashings," acts of police repression, riots, National Guard panics and killings. Some political activists have armed themselves for or against their fantasies of revolution — Panthers, Minutemen, Weathermen — and a

6

much larger number of people of quite divergent views have made their own private preparations for violence. There are a lot of guns in bureau drawers and back pockets. Our political language has turned violent. The old civilities — the alleged hypocrisies — of liberal intellectual discourse and political controversy have declined, are often condemned and despised. Hatred has been licensed in politics; people hate one another for political reasons, and they declare it and act it out. We are now a nation of pigs, snobs, traitors, Fascists, bums . . .

Beyond the frankly reactionary and avowedly revolutionary minorities, there is hostility between generations and subcultures, an antirationalist countercultural movement which has become, like revolution, an item of cultural fashion — "radical chic" — within the intelligentsia and the upper middle class. There is a popular movement against the waste and environmental corruption of industry and technology, a new phenomenon which has considerably more significance than appears on the surface. There is in all classes evidence of doubt, even despair, of the efficacy of political action: people are in reaction against what, for individual reasons, they see as the remoteness, impersonality, unaccountability — the incompetence — of liberal government as they know it today. There is a search for simplicities: revolution; a cathartic reordering of government; a new liberal, or illiberal, hero; a drastic reaffirmation of tradition, piety, authority, public morality.

I I

America is a special case, the hard case. It is the one country where government wages a foreign war for which a clear public mandate was never obtained. The Vietnam war distorts — it might even explain — a crisis which compounds other factors of political unrest and malfunction. Thus, to consider the liberal states as a whole — those of Western Europe, and North America as well — the question to be asked is whether the crisis is as deep as it obviously is wide. Is the public confidence easily recoverable? Is liberal political legitimacy, as such, in doubt, or simply the competence of certain governments, of recent Administrations, of existing party leaderships?

Optimism would be easier if politics were all that is involved. But the material and intellectual circumstances of modern life are drastically changing. Certain actualities and potentialities of technology — central war systems and the simplification of access to thermonuclear, chemical or bacteriological weapons of mass destruction, genetic control and manipulation, the social and political implications of drug use, the pace of information transmission and centralization, the development of "artificial intelligence," the impact of automation on industrial production and on the industrial labor force — have created a situation in which science and technology have come to be regarded as threats, while before they had seemed blessings. An anxiety about technology and industrialism which once was confined to a few conservative intellectuals and a few "reactionary" social groupings — peasants, the Church — now in another form is a dominant attitude among the liberal intelligentsia, to say nothing of the radical — as in Herbert Marcuse: "In the face of the totalitarian features of this society, the traditional notion of the 'neutrality' of technology can no longer be maintained. . . . the technological society is a system of domination which operated already in the concept and construction of techniques." Richard Nixon offers confirmation: the (industrial) pollution of our environment is "the issue of the 1970's."

Even without this reversal of attitudes toward technology, this cracking of the grounds for scientific optimism, technology and the growth in numbers of the Western populations had changed the conditions of Western political life in fundamental ways. In 1916 fewer than eighteen million Americans voted; in 1968 there were 73 million voters in a population twice that of a half-century earlier. In 1914, despite America's infatuation with the imperial idea — its scraps of empire picked up from enfeebled Spain, its Great White Ships and entrenched commercial-*cum*-political hegemony in Latin America — the United States was an isolated nation. There was no imperial class, and except among missionary Christian denominations little cult of foreign glamours or the uplift of lesser breeds. There was some reflected Rhodesian sentiment of Anglo-Saxon world supremacy, but most Americans were content to leave that to the British imperialists, toward whom they felt an ambivalent sense of kinship and the suspicion of victimization. We were a morally isolated nation. Today the United States has militarily, politically, and above all, morally implicated itself in what it chooses to define as a revolutionary upheaval of half the world's population.

We Americans have insisted upon seeing a unitary history for mankind, abjuring parochialism, but in so doing we have estranged ourselves from the moral framework, inevitably Western, which in the past made our political action intelligible to ourselves as well as to others, and which set some limits upon what we were

9

prepared to do. This generation of America's young is not simply the most anguished of our national experience but morally the most liberated; and this, it is necessary to say, has not simply freed them from sexual repressions and bourgeois hypocrisies but also made them capable of carrying out a massacre of civilians at My Lai. The moral universe they, and we, have rejected was a complex one.

The times, the velocity of history, set a condemnation upon that moral system, even if this is a revokable judgment — as it may or may not be. The interaction of politics and culture is such that political and moral legitimacies are related. Forty years ago painting, music and the professions were acknowledged to possess autonomous standards of integrity, so that a rejection of representational painting became at the same time an affirmation of the autonomy of art. There was — most of all among revolutionaries — moral reference to an absolute standard of social justice. Today justifications for revolutionary action and violence can possess the quality of antiesthetics, affirming an existential value for the actor which is indifferent to the consequences of the act and denies an intelligible reference to an external standard of justice.

America is the peculiar victim of what has been happening, and not only because of its own willed actions or the fact that it exists at the very edge of change, of constantly self-transforming industrial mass society. This country has a commitment to politics and a reliance upon politics which is without historical parallel. This is a consequence both of the colonial origins of this country and of its growth as an immigrant society — some forty million of Europe's ambitious, discontented and impoverished added to America's population in the century of the great immigrations. The individual as well as national identity of Americans has been affirmed in political terms. For the Frenchman or Hollander there are dimensions of national culture and experience which are indifferent to the character of the government of the moment. There is no distinction possible in America between *pays légal* and *pays réel,* between the state and the historical nation and culture. No nation existed here before the constitutional act of the eighteenth century. We have been compelled, for want of an alternative, to invest politics with heavy moral expectations, turning to politics for a kind of private as well as national fulfillment. The New Left today is profoundly American in its faith that politics can be redemptive, transforming man.

To expect so much of politics, to have so great a faith in political possibility, has also been a theme in recent European experience; it is a fundamental element in ideological politics. What is striking about the United States is the degree to which an unanalyzed historicism or political eschatology — no formal ideology — has affected popular beliefs about the American nation and its role in world affairs. The presidential rhetoric of American foreign policy, from Woodrow Wilson* to Richard

---

* And before. Wilson made the crucial modern formulation of an American missionary view of world affairs, but the sources lie in the founding experience of this nation as a new political dispensation, successor to Europe. Thus Thomas Jefferson: we are "the world's best hope." "Before the establishment of the American states nothing was known to history but the men of the old world, crowded within limits either small or overcharged, and steeped in the vices which that situation generates." It should be added that if Wilson initiated the modern period of American missionary internationalism, in the 1970's there is evidence of an awareness of the need to end or substantially modify it. But how? Reversal seems more plausible as the embittered outcome of national crisis and failure than a change through any act of national introspection and reappraisal.

Nixon, explicitly declares the United States to be a superior form of government and society, the essential pattern upon which the world — inevitably — will reform itself and come to share our advantages.

The practical expression of this attitude has been given two forms in our policy toward the rest of the world: the interventionist view, which sees America as obligated to act to bring about a fundamentally reformed world society, and the isolationist, which fears that the United States would corrupt itself by too close an involvement with others and which would have us set the national example for others to learn to emulate. Now there is a third attitude: that we still are unique, but in our crisis and our power to corrupt the rest of the world. The American New Left characteristically asserts that we are the *worst* nation in history, not merely one of a bad lot. The three views are alike in their assumption of American uniqueness, their conviction that we somehow have been and will continue to be spared the common lot of nations: the bloody-mindedness, but also the ordinariness, the predicaments and contradictions of action, the experience of failure.

At the same time our national experience provided obstacles to any very deep involvement in the experience of others. Physical and political isolation could reinforce moral isolation. Ours was the only conservative revolution, the only Enlightenment constitution to endure. Our national experience was of the frontier, of movement, of social innovation — of classlessness with its anxieties, of technological revolution and the exploitation of empty land and great national resources, the search for newness. American literature, reflecting this, has been parochial, turned inward, preoccupied with the search for place and identity in a situation of endless and treacherous flux. Even our greatest regionalist writer, dealing with our only regional culture of any permanence, William Faulkner, describes a society which cannot fix an order: the movement within the Mississippi border community still is radical and disruptive. The larger American experience, as it has been expressed in nearly all of our literature, is with breaking free, with the ambiguity of inevitable success.

Lincoln could say to a caller, ". . . you flaxen men with broad faces are born with cheer, and don't know a cloud from a star. I am of another temperament." He spoke from out of the only American experience of national tragedy. But the Civil War was a hundred years ago, and our wars since then have been insouciant adventures. Even World War II was an adventure for us, although it was thick with catastrophes for all of the other participants. Vietnam has ended a casual century for Americans.

I I I

I say all of this because it seems to me that what is crucially new in the situation of the United States today is that we confront not simply a crisis of government and policy but a refutation of certain fundamental assumptions about ourselves, about others in their relationship to the United States, and about the role and competence of politics. Our confidence in ourselves is shaken — our moral confidence, but also our belief in our practical competence to win wars, manage our economy, reform the structure of our own and others' societies, manage technology and make ideas work. We are severely shaken in our faith in American social stability. Our national violence and the social fissures revealed these last half-dozen years have undermined a characteristic — and indispensable — American optimism. We have in some degree come to fear ourselves, our potentialities, and this is not simply a matter affecting the liberal (or radical) intelligentsia. It affects that considerably larger number of Americans responsible for our crisis of legitimacy — that is to say, responsible for a popular withdrawal of confidence in the government's competence to rule, to redress injustice.

Moral attitudes and perceptions underlie our politics. American national policy clearly has rested in a very wide consensus of popular opinion regarding the merits of liberal representative government and the free economy as against alternative systems. In Western Europe, domestic politics as well as the alliance with America reflected a kindred moral judgment. Now there is a clear weakening of this moral consensus. Doubt has emerged within the United States not only about the wisdom of our present policies but about the validity of a whole series of political and social assumptions fundamental to the present form of American government. In Western Europe there are not only a questioning of American situation — of the competence of American government, and the quality and stability of American society — but a parallel movement of reaction against certain aspects of Europe's own liberal governments.

In Europe, too, the issues of political accountability of modern government, its ability to solve — even to define — certain urgently felt social and political issues, its competence, its responsiveness to popular anxieties, have become important. Since the famous Paris Spring of 1968 there has been some provisional quieting of domestic controversies, but, one would imagine, only that. The problems remain acute, and they are problems of governmental responsiveness to deep issues of social dislocation, "modern" issues of life in industrial society. We encounter a new radical critique of industrial and liberal society, a revival of "*Weltanschauung* politics."

There is popular discontent with the programs and performances of the major political parties; there is the development of an antirationalist intellectual movement, political withdrawal or "privatism" among many people from ordinarily politically active classes and social sectors, a widespread expression of a sense of frustration, impotence, in the face of anonymous, authoritarian and unresponsive power structures, a fear of what technological progress is bringing about, a new distrust of "expert" judgment, caused by a series of social failures or policy blunders underwritten by expert counsel, and thus a reaction against the established leadership classes and groups within the Western nations. In summary it can be said that there are rebellions against many of the conditions of contemporary life in the Western industrial nations, against political and social policies which seem to create or perpetuate those conditions, and against the values underlying those policies.

We must, then, consider whether this new situation actually expresses basic anxieties related to the developing conditions of urban-industrial life in the West. If this were true, are the existing structures of liberal democratic politics and government competent to acknowledge and deal with these anxieties? Or are new forces and structures — evolutionary, or by default, revolutionary — inevitable? Are our intellectual categories relevant to this situation? Or may we be applying certain assumptions of a "modern" age — of Enlightenment optimism about the historical process, scientific optimism, pragmatic parliamentarian and competitive politics — to a "postmodern" situation as yet inchoate? Might we be at a point in Western history where the structural relationship of individuals to state power and to the material resources available to organized society needs to be rethought under the pressures of new popular anxieties, new issues of personal identity, political community, and ambivalence toward rationalist values and technological progress?

Our problem is not merely that war, social tension or a new radicalism disturbs the Western nations today; the problem is to discover the nature of anxieties and political failures underlying this discontent, which is expressed in one way by the New Left but in another — less articulate but perhaps more significant — manner by people who have nothing to do with the New Left, or even abominate it as one cause of their own alienation. There is a New Populism today as well as a New Left. The two are not challenge and reaction, but a single movement signifying despair of liberalism.

CHAPTER II

Social
Dissolution

. . . we are witnessing an enormous dislocation of something that can now be hardly seen or heard, but which has been wisdom. Of that wisdom there is nothing left but "scattered limbs." What I mean is this: obviously, the technical processes which have been so prodigiously developed and specialized during the past half century have as their aim the rational ordering of all the resources at the disposal of mankind; a whole body of recipes is growing up as to the detailed manner of this ordering. Yet if we ask ourselves what is the connection between this body — so vast that it has in it the material of countless manuals — and what used to be known as wisdom, we will see that it is only its residue, its left-over, its dregs. You could put it like this: the huge multiplication of means put at man's disposal, and of recipes for their use, takes place at the cost of the ends they are supposed to serve, or, if you like, at the cost of the values which man is called upon both to serve and to safeguard. It is as if man, over-burdened by the weight of technics, knows less and less where he stands in regard to what matters to him and what doesn't, to what is precious and what is worthless.

— Gabriel Marcel

I

IT IS THE LUXURY of
the middle-class intellectual to articulate such feelings as
alienation, estrangement, anomie. But these anxieties are
real experiences for a great many ordinary citizens of the
Western industrial societies today. An examination of why
people are in retreat from their commitment to the liberal
state and economy — the modern system — must begin
with the fact and scale of modern-day change: drastic
change, of unprecedented velocity, imposed upon the
lives of millions of people by technology, social mobility
and urbanization.

The process is not new; it has been the common experience in much of the West for a century. Yet we too easily
ignore that the human degradations caused by industrialization did not end when Keynesian theory and the mixed
economy supplanted the indiscriminately savage free-
market orthodoxies of nineteenth- and early-twentieth-
century capitalism. The condition of life for America's
modern subproletariat of the inner cities, driven from the
farms by the industrialization of agricultural production,
or of the remaining migrant proletariat of the factory
farms, too often illiterate, incompetent to function in an
economy of skilled specialized trades, time clocks, written instructions, is fully comparable to that of nineteenth-century England's uprooted and discarded agricultural proletariat. Then the recourse was nihilistic
drunkenness; today in the urban ghetto it is heroin. As it

was then, life is now brutalized, stripped of the social framework and popular culture which accompanied and in some degree mitigated traditional agricultural poverty. Poverty, in Ivan Illich's phrase, has been "modernized," despite the institutional attempts to deal with it. "The poor have always been socially powerless. The increasing reliance on institutional care adds a new dimension to their new helplessness: psychological impotence, the inability to fend for themselves."

In Western Europe the new proletariat of Turkish, South European and North African industrial workers — men without their families, housed in barracks or *bidonvilles* — at least have jobs and are engaged in an intelligible economic struggle, lifting themselves to a new level, but they also constitute a segregated and politically powerless class, an industrial helotry. Still, they are the lucky ones, compared with the all but hopelessly disabled ranks among the American migrants to the city. As Illich adds of the United States, "nowhere else is poverty treated at greater cost. Nowhere else does the treatment of poverty produce so much dependence, anger, frustration, and further demands. And nowhere else should it be so evident that poverty — once it has become modernized — has become resistant to treatment with dollars alone."

The very poor admittedly are a special problem, but what is hard to admit is that they may constitute a characteristic problem of advanced industrialism. Modern industrial society rewards particular talents and abilities, a conceptual imagination, a verbal intelligence, mechanical skills and insight, the ability to work by routine and in disciplined groups. These skills are different from those valued in the agricultural society, from which most of today's poor are recruited, and cannot always be learned, nor is everyone capable of learning them. The peasant community, to take the exceptional case, tolerates and may even provide an economic role for its village idiot: the industrial society ruthlessly discards him, or institutionalizes him — which is to say, locks him up.

All of this must be acknowledged without romanticizing preindustrial society, which is in any event wholly unrecapturable. But the costs, certain of the structural characteristics and demands of industrial society, must be viewed realistically and not avoided as somehow untypical discrepancies or easily remedied lapses in a fundamentally benign progressive development of society. More time and more money will not inevitably bring the discards of modern society up to the general level of prosperity and productive life. It may actually seal their fate as new outcastes.

But the accomplishments of industrial society are manifest. There is a striking passage in Anthony West's novel *Heritage,* where the young hero of the book, like the author (West is the son of H. G. Wells), is the son of a famous and self-made prophet of the scientific age. The young man gives voice to a mood of romantic adolescent rejection of the vulgarity and materialism of a London Christmas Eve street scene of the 1930's. The father replies:

> You've no idea how decent the London crowd is, compared with what it was when I was a youngster. . . . It was a vile town when I came to it as a boy. The streets were just as jammed as they are now, but it was all horse-drawn traffic, drays, carts, delivery vans and buses. We lived in the reek of a dirty stable all the time. The streets were covered with an unspeakable slime. You don't know how lucky you are to live in a motor age. The smell of burnt oil and gas

isn't nice, but you've no idea of the smells we had to
live with. People smelt then, in a way they don't now.
Nice people had baths, but the poor just didn't. They
washed their faces and hands and they went to bed in
their underclothes. I don't know when pajamas, cheap
pajamas, came in, but they didn't exist when I was a
boy. Not for my sort anyway. On a holiday night like
this the streets were filled with a crowd that stank of
stale sweat. And we all wore such horrible clothes, made
of cheap serges and ugly materials, and we had to put
up with such beastly clumsy boots. You don't realize
what a liberation cheap shoes have meant . . . and
all these cheap amusements. There was nothing to do
if you wanted a bit of fun except going to the pub, the
boozer. People drank themselves silly. If we'd walked
through the streets like this on Christmas Eve when I
was your age, half the people we met would have been
staggering drunk. We would have seen a dozen men
and women throwing up in the gutters. And fights —
you've no idea how disgustingly they used to fight, full
of cheap gin and beer, you'd see women fighting each
other in a circle of laughing louts.

This change took place in the years between 1884 (when
H. G. Wells actually came up to London from the provinces) and the 1930's. Cheap pajamas and cheap shoes,
baths and decent housing for the masses of people, cheap
amusements — not bad to be able to make such a judgment on fifty years of social change. And we must add:
pensions, good food, medicine, dentists for the poor. In
Wells's own England the very physical quality of the race
has been transformed within this century. The dark,
scrawny English workingman, with his stinking decayed
teeth and chronic illnesses, the worse of Disraeli's two
nations, now is vanishing — vanishing considerably faster
than the servility and class-obsession which provide his
inherited psychological disablement.

I I

Then, what about these people, who, in fundamental matters of ordinary life, have been the great beneficiaries of modern industrial and urban society? Their gain is the value which we can set against the fate of industrialism's casualties. Yet they, rather than the modernized poor, provide the New Populists, restless with the established forms of liberal government and economy, notoriously vulnerable to the appeal of antiliberal movements.* The origin of Europe's prewar Fascist movements among adventurers and *déclassé* intellectuals, the beer-hall and street-fighting aura of early Fascism and Nazism, have contributed to a widespread assumption that Fascism was a movement of the unassimilated *Lumpenproletariat* of industrial society, or of a *Lumpenproletariat* being manipulated by capitalist oligarchs and militarists. Actually, in 1921 the Italian Fascist party numbered half as many more members from the middle and professional classes as from the proletariat. The Nazi party had a majority in most German universities before it was a major popular movement. The Hungarian Fascist party (the Arrow Cross) in 1937 was more than half industrial workers — "blue collar" — in membership, more than a quarter professional men. (Only peasants typically were greatly underrepresented in the European Fascist movements;

---

* A European scholar, Torcuato S. Di Tella, comments: "Populism is widespread when the Tocquevillean 'intermediate associations' are weak or nonexistent. Populism provides, then, a *short cut* to social change, replacing the very complex and difficult process of mass organization by more primitive alternatives. Instead of an ideology, the personality cult and charisma; instead of grass-roots leadership and financial contributions, a superimposed structure of military men and wealthy financiers, the origin of whose money is not always clear."

peasant rebellions historically have tended to be reactionary — antiurban and antilandlord.) The Fascist movements, at least in their earlier years of struggle for power, voiced a powerful and classless appeal for social "revolution" as a means to social reintegration. In George L. Mosse's words: "All fascisms attempted to capture and direct bourgeois dissatisfaction with existing industrial and political reality, a dissatisfaction which began to take concrete revolutionary form in the late nineteenth century. . . . Fascism was against conventions, but on another level it attempted to find a new sense of 'belonging' that might be combined with the revolt."

Because of the vast material improvement brought about in the lives of millions, today's Western industrial society has been described as the society of affluence. This says too much; it is clear that affluence is unevenly distributed, riddled with irrationalities, and that even for its beneficiaries it creates its own new demands and pressures. Yet the new demands are of a rather different urgency than those of the past, and the great beneficiaries of this affluence have been the ordinary organized industrial worker and the middle classes of the Western nations. The French industrial workingman may be hard pressed to support his family, but he is supporting them at a level of material well-being far above that of his father's family, and the threat over him no longer is quite the same threat of family ruin or starvation. (For the Algerian laborer working in metropolitan France, as for the South Carolina farm laborer in America, it may still be another matter.) The American white-collar worker typically is heavily mortgaged, deeply committed in consumer credit, but the absolute improvement in his living standard and social security since World War II is very high, and he knows it.

Yet economic struggle has been the fundamental orienting force in modern Western politics. The great political conflicts and party issues of the last two hundred years in Western society have been economic and class issues. Now — and perhaps this will prove an ephemeral characteristic, an illusion, of the 1950's and 1960's, perhaps not — the economic struggle has for the mainstream of the Western society lost its old and terrible urgency. People are better off; they expect to become still better off; and they do not expect that a national economic crisis or breakdown will be allowed to ruin them. The problem of popular economic well-being *seems*, for the mass of people in the West, at least *potentially soluble*. This is the real significance of the "affluent society," and it discloses a profound shift in popular expectations of government — a near-revolutionary transformation in the political imagination, the political culture, of the West.

It has also meant that people have encountered — and found it possible to admit — anxieties which before were obscured. What can be described as the "new" anxieties of contemporary society — anxieties of private identity, of meaning and creativity in industrial and bureaucratic work, of affirming a significance to life in the aftermath, or default, of the value systems and allegiances and religious commitments of the past — have certainly existed before now, but they were also overridden by the simple struggle to survive. Who am I? Posing such a question would have been an inconceivable luxury to a Ruhr miner or Manchester laborer of the years before 1900. I do not mean to suggest that the workingman of the present day typically

exists in a state of existential self-examination. I do mean
that he finds himself living at a point in time when, however uneasily, he enjoys an unprecedented relaxation of
the most urgent demands of economic survival, and at
the same time (and in a direct relationship to this release)
he finds the community and class bonds, the value structures, the social and religious coherence of society, falling
away from him. He finds the value of his craft diminished
by technological change, "the social status and market
value" of his skills reduced, to quote a 1970 U.S. Labor
Department report to the White House. That report
added that the some seventy million white Americans
with incomes between $5,000 and $10,000 a year "were
no less dissatisfied than the students with the conditions
of American society"; they were "overripe for a political
response to the pressing needs they feel so keenly." The
new industrial worker's economic security has presented
a bill: the cost is in social disillusion and moral disorientation, and it is a heavy cost.

The great imperative of economic survival is diminished for a major part of the population, and with it a
profound principle of social reality may be weakened.
Sigmund Freud's observation was that for most people,
work is the most important agency binding them to reality. The extraordinary fantasies, cults, fears, dreamlike
misunderstandings which gain some political articulation
and credence in our society, or are acted out in assassinations, revolutionary and counterrevolutionary murders
and bombings, the organization of conspiratorial under-
ground groups on right and left, can only suggest the
lurid landscape in which our secret imaginations function.
The millennial fantasies of the past are fairly well known
— fantasies of elites, as in the *illuminati* and "secret knowl-

edge" cults of the Middle Ages and the Enlightenment, chiliastic peasant crusades and "religions of the oppressed," the millennial cryptopolitical upheavals of uprooted or economically displaced townsmen. Norman Cohn writes that, typically, apocalyptic fantasies have flourished among "people [who] lacked the material and emotional support afforded by traditional social groups; their kinship groups had disintegrated." They are, he says, rootless men "in the midst of a society where traditional norms and relationships are disintegrating."

The totalitarian parties of this century, our contemporary expressions of the popular quest for revolutionary salvation, all have included a promise of social reintegration, re-creating an identity for individuals freed, or torn loose, from the old fixities of place, class, custom, of inherited status and role. The *Communist Manifesto* accurately described the modern process of disruption and disintegration, describing it — not without a note of grudging admiration — as the work of the bourgeoisie. Marx and Engels wrote:

> The bourgeoisie cannot exist without constantly revolutionising the instruments of production, and thereby the relations of production and with them the whole relations of society. Conservation of the old modes of production in unaltered form was, on the contrary, the first condition of existence for all earlier industrial classes. Constant revolutionising of production, uninterrupted disturbance of all social conditions, everlasting uncertainty and agitation distinguish the bourgeois epoch from all earlier ones. All fixed, fast frozen relations, with their train of ancient and venerable prejudices and opinions, are swept away, all new-formed ones become antiquated before they can ossify. All that is solid melts into air, all that is holy is profaned, and man is at last compelled to face with sober senses his

real conditions of life and his relations with his kind. . . .

The bourgeoisie, by the rapid improvement of all instruments of production, by the immensely facilitated means of communication, draws all, even the most barbarian, nations into civilisation. The cheap prices of its commodities are the heavy artillery with which it batters down all Chinese walls, with which it forces the barbarians' intensely obstinate hatred of foreigners to capitulate. It compels all nations, on pain of extinction, to adopt the bourgeois mode of production; it compels them to introduce what it calls civilisation into their midst, i.e., to become bourgeois themselves. In a word, it creates a world after its own image.

The *Manifesto* calls the revolution in technology the work of the bourgeoisie. But the technological revolution itself — if we understood it as a revolutionary change in the minds and intention of men, an adoption of *technique* — possesses an autonomous claim to the prime role as agent of social revolution. The merchant and entrepreneurial middle classes sometimes dominated the process and profited by the result, and sometimes — as in modern Russia, Cuba and China — they were themselves the victims of a ruthless social transformation whose essential characteristics have proved largely indifferent to the political auspices under which they function. Jacques Ellul, for example, argues that "technological society" — which this passage from Marx and Engels could as well have been describing — resulted from the coincidence of several factors at the end of the eighteenth and the beginning of the nineteenth centuries: the maturing of machine techniques themselves, population growth, a suitable economic milieu, "the almost complete plasticity of a society malleable and open to the propagation of technique," and an eventual clear and conscious intention to combine and direct these forces to a technical objective.

This "plasticity" of the society is crucial. The French revolutionary period inaugurated the era of technological society, with religion unseated and philosophical materialism affirmed; with various established hierarchies and natural groups — guilds, communes, as well as the privileges of parliament and the universities — successfully attacked, including the family unit. Ellul writes: "The individual remained the sole sociological unit. . . . For the individual in an atomized society, only the state was left: the state was the highest authority and it became omnipotent as well. The society produced was perfectly malleable and remarkably flexible from both the intellectual and the material points of view. The technical phenomenon had its most favorable environment since the beginning of history."

I I I

In our time, the 1970's, this social dissolution is far advanced with an alternative social integration unachieved. The old prerevolutionary, pretechnological society — the "idiocy of rural life," as Marx had it — survived into the twentieth century for major segments of the Western populations. Only since World War II has the grip of agrarian society finally been broken in France, the United States and Germany; in England the aristocratic social myth, the power over the English imagination exercised by the ideal of country life and of a rural gentry, still lingers, but its social basis is all but gone. In Italy the process is accomplished in the north, under way in the south.

Moreover, the nineteenth century's means for social reintegration of the working people — working-class solidarity and socialist political mobilization — has itself become the victim of affluence, consumer society, the promotion of the old industrial laboring classes into that classless middle class which is the most important new feature of the social landscape. The great social phenomenon of the wartime and postwar years in Western Europe and the United States has been mobility: physical mobility and class mobility.

In Europe the war itself caused the uprooting of some 30 million people from their home soil and home communities. Immediately after the war another 25 million were shifted, and 15 million Germans have subsequently moved from East to West Germany. In the 1950's and 1960's — years of the recruitment of South European, North African and Turkish workers to industry in West Germany, France, Switzerland and the Italian North — additional millions were affected annually. In the 1960's some 100,-000 to 125,000 seasonal workers came to France annually, the largest numbers from Spain, Portugal and North Africa. In 1966 Germany had an immigration, both long-term and short, of over 700,000. Switzerland had nearly 300,000 immigrants, most of them short-term workers (and in 1970 underwent a sharp nationalist popular reaction against immigration on this scale). Between 1950 and 1968, nearly a million Spaniards migrated to other European states. In 1968, 222,000 Italians migrated abroad — a figure approaching one half of one percent of the total Italian population of 54 million — and another 1,500,000 migrated within Italy, most of them from the south, or 3 percent of the population, a rate of internal migration which was fairly constant throughout the 1960's in Italy.

In the United States the Great Depression, World War II, and postwar economic expansion between them, attracted or compelled millions of Americans into a migration which, while it was not unprecedented in quality in this country of restless movement to new lands in the West and to the frontier, nonetheless broke down towns and farming settlements made in the late nineteenth and early twentieth centuries in the Midwest and Great Plains, and in the South. The agricultural depression, the great dust storms of the 1930's, the subsequent mechanization of agriculture, in forty years reduced the agricultural labor force in this country from 27 percent of the working population to 8.9 percent. The new war industries set up in the 1940's in the Southwest and on the West Coast, and the conversion to war production of the established manufacturing industries of the North Central States, attracted a huge migration. Los Angeles went from a 577,000 population in 1920 to 2,800,000 in 1970 — a 450 percent increase (when total U.S. population was doubling). The portion of the American population living in rural areas dropped from half in 1920 to less than a third in 1960, and of that third far fewer are actually engaged in agriculture. The mortality of industries forced a steady, if less dramatic, labor movement out of the obsolete mills of the East, the declining mines, into the newer manufactures. While Southern California and Dallas and the Boston-Cambridge areas were growing, such towns as New Bedford, Scranton and Wheeling were experiencing an absolute decline.

For individuals these moves might only have been from one New England town to another, from a closed shoe-manufacturing plant in Massachusetts or a hatter's factory in Danbury to an aircraft or electronic or optical plant, or it might have been a move to the South or to the West Coast. Or more often the move was made by sons and daughters while their fathers bleakly took relief, or social security, or odd jobs, in a sepulchral town of the old and discarded. In each case it meant a fatal break in the continuity of a local social structure, a social organism whose life extended back into the nineteenth century, and the movement of people into new communities made up of nuclear families — often enough (especially in new housing in the vast, newly developed areas like Long Island or the Los Angeles complex) families of a uniform age with a uniform level of income and doing related kinds of work.

This physical mobility of Americans from the 1930's through the 1970's has constituted social mobility. These have been workers and their families moving to — or searching for — better jobs, moving to improve their lot, sending their children to community colleges or state universities, steadily discarding the evidences of past poverty and class origin, the accents and attitudes of their parents, becoming or striving to become members of the new American class of the classless.

They have been the successful modern migrants. As the migrant poor have experienced a cultural as well as geographic immigration from rural poverty to "modernized" urban poverty, these families have lifted themselves into a "modernized" and amorphous American middle class characterized by an admirable ambition and courage, and also a notorious anomie. It is an insecure class, cohering on a fragile nexus of national patriotism, all that survives of the old web of community.

In Europe, by contrast, the transnational worker migrations involve little social transformation; in the majority of cases the immigrants have remained in the lower ranks of labor, sharply vulnerable to unemployment, and they have not expected to achieve a new status in the new place but simply in the end to return home with some capital for a shop or farm or for retirement. Very often this has also been true for population movements within the European nations. Mobility in Europe is not producing a classlessness on the American analogy. Using access to national political power as an index of upward social mobility, the Italian sociologist Alessandro Pizzarno has argued that while the European working classes and lower middle classes have steadily improved their chances for attaining formal political power over several decades, this appears to have had much more to do with the consequences of universal suffrage than with class mobility or the overturning of class barriers. (Fifteen years after the British Labour party came to power in 1945, seemingly leading a movement which would abolish the class bar, the group holding power in Britain proved to have come from an even narrower and "much more class-conditioned category" than those who governed before World War II. Today, after a second Labour government, led by university dons and middle-class intellectuals, the Conservative party is back in power with a prime minister of working-class origins who nonetheless is a yachtsman in possession of an Oxford education and an Albany flat, with a cabinet made up of old Etonians, ex-officers of the Household Brigade, company directors, and solicitors.)

In the matter of economic change among European workers, while there is an obvious new affluence and a new premium on technocratic competence and technical education in the middle and upper-middle levels of European business management, Pizzarno concludes that "despite the dynamism which characterizes the economic life of this postwar period, the group wielding the economic power remains exclusive and virtually inaccessible." Thus Europe has had popular mobility and migration without the degree of class mobility attained in the United States. The effect of migration and physical mobility has been the undermining of old social structures and communities. The effect of class mobility is the creation of a socially *déraciné* population increasingly cut off from the solidarity afforded (at whatever cost) by strong class consciousness. But if the mobile and newly affluent European worker continues to identify himself as working-class, and residually — often in a reactionary state of mind — with a political party of workingmen, the other side of that coin remains frustration, the choking off of young talent, resentments that find their own political expressions.

I V

There is an additional reason for emphasizing the new mobility of Western society and the pace of urbanization as factors creating a new condition in Western political culture. The United States and to a lesser extent the West European societies are becoming urban civilizations. As Irving Kristol writes: "In terms of the *quality* of American life, the United States is now one vast metropolis. Cities are nothing new; the problems of cities are nothing new; but an urban civilization is very new indeed, and the problems of an urban civilization are without precedent in human history." The old tension between city and country has been resolved by the disintegration of nonurban culture and values, the liquidation of the provincial nation as a decisive force in the national imagination and in shaping the national culture. There is in classical political philosophy, including the federalist philosophy of America's eighteenth-century origins, an abiding distrust of the city as populated by uprooted and economically dependent masses (not primary producers, but suppliers of labor and services): a crowd, potentially a mob, rather than a democratic people. Kristol goes on to say:

> The interesting consideration is the extent to which a mob is not simply a physical presence but also, and above everything else, a state of mind. It is, to be precise, that state of mind which lacks all of those qualities that, in the opinion of the founding fathers, added up to republican morality: steadiness of character, deliberativeness of mind, and a mild predisposition to subordinate one's own special interests to the public interest. Since the founding fathers could not envisage a nation of bourgeois — a nation of urbanized, prosperous, and strongly acquisitive citizens — they located republican morality in the agrarian sector of American life. We, in this century, have relocated it in the suburban and small city sector of American life— our contemporary version of America's "grass roots." And it now appears that our anticipations may be treated as roughly by history as were those of the founding fathers.

This urbanization of the Western nations has been accompanied by a decisive centralization of authority. The processes have coincided. To a considerable extent, although not an inevitable one (as the Swiss cantonal system demonstrates, in the obvious case), the one has caused the other. The result has been to gather power into agencies more and more remote from the individual at the same time that the individual's own political role is diminished. His political power has been interrupted by more and more intermediary mechanisms; his command over national decisions is more indirect than ever because of the introduction of layers of experts and specialists while at the same time the impact of the central political power has been explosively enlarged — its power over the national economy, its war-making power and weaponry, its information about the lives of citizens, its knowledge of economics, social organization, and technology.

Nongovernmental centers of power have experienced a comparable growth and centralization. The power of the great industries, trusts and cartels of the nineteenth century and the years before World War I, selfish and socially irresponsible, cannot compare with the power exercised by today's national and international economic entities, politically regulated as they may be. And while the regulation of these enterprises has forced them into policies consistent with the interests and values of the Western governments, it does not follow that the invidious impact upon the individual citizen of their power and decisions has been lessened. The individual, perhaps more than ever, is the powerless bystander. At times he is the beneficiary, at times the victim of decisions made by the managers of great economic entities and their collaborators in the regulatory agencies of the national governments and international financial agencies. Collectively, in the mass, his plight or his well-being may force changes in the policies of national and international economic management. As an individual he is helpless; and more important, the power of his designated political representative — his congressman, his parliamentary deputy — is diminished. It is diminished by no plot of the financiers and "the bosses," but mainly by the new scale of the problems, the new sophistication of knowledge demanded in managing the economy. The subordination of the free economy to political decision — to "democratic decision" — has in fact accelerated the centralization of power in the hands of economic specialists and the professional managers who alone seem to possess the relevant knowledge.

Indeed, to possess relevant knowledge has itself become much more difficult in all fields. The geometrical proliferation of scientific and technological data, and the parallel development of data and theory in economics and the social disciplines, narrows the ability of people to master what they should, or think they should, know. Much of this "progress" in knowledge is waste or irrelevance; nevertheless, it presents a formidable problem of discrimination. In the sciences — by definition, areas of cumulative knowledge — work becomes more and more specialized, and the acquisition of a generalist's knowledge, a policy maker's and serious politician's knowledge, becomes that much harder. Wisdom — a quality which resists positive definition and quantification — is at a discount in the regime of expertise.*

And to what goal is this centralized and enlarged knowledge and power applied? Our malaise is most keen in exactly this matter of value and objective. As short a time ago as ten years — the start of the Kennedy era, when

---

* The contemporary confirmation of this case is provided by Vietnam, where an American elite has tirelessly applied specialized knowledge, "hard" knowledge, the positivist social sciences, the most sophisticated technological intelligence, in defiance of common sense. It was the common sense of the American public in 1964 and 1965 that a land war in Asia against an insurgent movement within a politically tormented and fragile state was not a good idea. The experts knew better.

the political optimism of the West soared — it was possible to believe in the inevitability of social and political progress, the susceptibility of disorder to reasoned reorder, the confident power of political mind and action. The contradictions which that American Administration met were in part the fault of its own hubris, in part the blows of incalculable events; yet the terrible climax in Dallas provided, in retrospect, a symbolic assassination of hope for Americans and a confirmation of frustrations that were already being felt internationally. Some people today still cling to the belief that what has happened since 1963 is a matter of bad men, bad leaders, with the old beliefs easily recoverable under a new version of liberal political leadership. Perhaps this is a necessary optimism; yet the truth, as masses of people see it, is probably closer to what Jo Grimond, the British Liberal party leader, has written: that this kind of confidence no longer exists. "No longer is it simply a question of getting the right people into the White House, or Downing Street. A change of party is seen . . . simply as a matter of protest, not an affirmation of confidence in a different set of steersmen at the controls. The machine itself is suspect . . . moreover, there is a creeping realization that the orthodox, the superior, the complacent 'experts' are nearly always wrong on all major issues."

Yet the "experts" have always been wrong. Cynicism about the political intelligence of experts is a prime lesson of history. Until recently, this cynicism could be combined with a faith in the ultimately favorable outcome of a free play of the ideas and forces of the intellectual and political marketplace. There was an ultimate confidence in the benignity of the historical process, a confidence which since the Enlightenment has survived all attack from reactionary philosophers, Christian or Stoic pessimists, the literary prophets of disintegration. In the nineteenth century, Baudelaire could ask in his journal if "it is not specifically in political matters that the universal ruin or the universal progress — for the name matters little — will be manifested. That will appear in the degradation of the human heart. Need I describe how the last vestiges of statesmanship will struggle painfully in the last clutches of a universal bestiality, how the Governors will be forced — in maintaining themselves and erecting a phantom of order — to resort to measures which would make our men of today shudder . . . ? The world is about to end . . . so far will progress have atrophied in us all that is spiritual, that no dream of the Utopians, however bloody, sacrilegious, or unnatural, will be comparable to the result."

Borne out by the cataclysm of World War I and its aftermath, this kind of warning still was not really heard by the people of the liberal West. There was in the 1920's and 1930's a sinister popular shift from reason to unreason, from the old politics to a new politics of redemptive Bolshevik or Fascist revolution — optimism translated into a higher and more desperate pitch of action — and that was a sign of the neurotic self-doubt of Western liberal society. Yet the general optimism remained pervasive, even in the face, twenty-five years after the first war, of Treblinka and Buchenwald.

It remained pervasive, but with seams of doubt. The strongest component in the historical optimism of the West was provided by the unmistakable evidence that ordinary men's lives were being bettered: this evidence could offset the unprecedented crimes of twentieth-century governments, and the effect of those crimes upon the "ordinary lives" of those millions who became victims. GNP growth, worker prosperity, cheap cars and homes for the masses, were purported to be the characteristic product of liberal industrial society. The manufacture of terror and war was an aberration. Faith in social progress seemed warranted by the fact of scientific and technological progress. Western historical optimism has expressed a deep conviction that the mind of man is capable of laying open the problems of society, finding practical solutions whose cumulative effect steadily improves the common lot, just as the mind of man has laid open the realities of the physical universe. The drama of scientific progress, moving men's knowledge of physical nature in three centuries from next to nil to the mastery of space, the atom, human illness, human genetics, was understood to be the analogue of social possibility, a comparable God-like mastery by man of man himself. Always this has been challenged, doubted, but always it has been in the air — an assumption of Western society which, even if we feared that it might not bear too close an examination, nonetheless animated our lives, our politics.

But now the scientific and technological analogue of progress is discredited. A belief in the unalloyed beneficence of science has been increasingly hard to hold since that July day in 1945 when Robert Oppenheimer witnessed the first atomic explosion and self-consciously declared that he had made himself into Kali, the god of destruction. Since then, for all our ritual proclamation of the dangers of the nuclear age, we have largely repressed our knowledge of what this really meant. We have constructed huge nuclear military forces, and made nuclear threats and planned for the eventualities of nuclear war, in a condition of emotional denial, of "nuclear incredulity" — even savagely denigrating those few who provocatively thought "unthinkable" thoughts and suggested to us exactly what we were about. But the worm of truth was there, and today it is with some real sense of relief that important elements in the Western publics have suddenly turned against technology, against "pollution," against the whole range of scientifically and technologically induced threats to human society for which nuclear weapons provide the prototype.

The old orienting Western values of religion, dynastic rule, traditional community, had become the victims of scientific rationalism and skepticism, but for nearly all the modern era, science was without skepticism about itself. It confidently promised a new series of secular values for Western society: and now these display inner contradiction. Scientific warrant had been given for a new view of society as in progress, experiencing an ultimately redemptive progressive development analogous to technological progress. This has in quite recent times been contradicted in the eyes of masses of people by the evident "reversions" and crimes of scientific society — mass industrialized warfare, genocide — and now the analogue itself is unseated. If the Enlightenment closed the doors of hell, as George Steiner has remarked, by making sin lead not to punishment but to redemption, the significance of the "ecological crisis" as a popular issue would seem to be that those gates have been reopened under new management. Or to quote Leszek Kolakowski, technological civilization had created "a false irreligiosity which arises not from the overcoming of religious symbols as a way of thought, but from stifling the self-awareness of the situation which gives birth to religious symbols," and now that solution is being denied us. But since we have discarded our belief in immortality we again face the inveterate temptation of Western politics, to attach to political action that possibility — of redemption — which before was understood to lie outside time.

CHAPTER III

The Burst Structures of Liberal Society

Many scientific theories have, for very long periods of time, stood the test of experience until they had to be discarded owing to man's decision, not merely to make other experiments, but to have different experiences.

— Eric Heller

I

THE LIBERAL political
system was the creation of a Western society lunar in its
remoteness from us. Representative government — with
a free play of ideas and of contending individuals and
interest groups within a "contractual" agreement to accept the will of the majority, the guarantee of certain
"unalienable" rights to all — was largely the creation of
a very small elite of classically educated eighteenth-
century intellectuals. Its success was inaugurated
within agrarian societies possessing governments whose
range of competence and involvement in the national
life were drastically more limited than ours. The great
Italian historian Guglielmo Ferrero may reasonably argue
that the famous proclamation of national mobilization
in the French revolutionary wars — reflecting the furious
moralism and application of Terror of the Revolution itself — inaugurated, in principle at least, the modern state
and the contemporary practice of totalitarian government.*

* The declaration read: "Young men will go forth to battle; married
men will forge weapons and transport munitions; women will make tents
and clothing, and serve in hospitals; children will make bandages from
old linen; and old men will be brought to the public squares to arouse
the courage of the soldiers, while preaching the unity of the Republic
and hatred against kings." Ferrero comments: "The young revolutionaries embarked on a bold adventure, full of danger, during which, at a
certain moment, they were seized by fear; and impelled by fear, they
overstepped the limits which their predecessors had learned to respect.
If the Revolution did much evil, the reason was that at a certain moment . . . in the madness of fear it believed it had discovered a new
art of warfare, a new diplomacy, a new policy, which were nothing but
illusions about the power of force . . . to oblige men to be free. . . .

Yet the density and complexity of ordinary modern
state power and bureaucratic involvement with the citizenry (to say nothing of the Stalinist and Nazi states)
barely admit of a practical comparison. Even Napoleonic
state reform and the creation of the modern centralized
apparatus of civil service could not turn agrarian France
into a mass society—even television and the twentieth
century have not quite been able to do that. Italy, notorious for its parasitic bureaucracy and impenetrable mass
of civil law and procedure, remains famously individualistic to this day, actually governed in crucial respects by
social codes, local traditions and moral assumptions that
are the powerful inheritance of an Italian *culture* which
traditionally has paid little heed to the state, liberal or
otherwise, except as the state provides an arena for the
playing out of individual roles. The Italian liberal state
was in some sense obsolescent from the time it was established, adapted from foreign models and imposed by an
elite upon a society whose organic political life was regional. The national difficulties of Italy today derive in
considerable part from this anachronism in the relationship of institutions to reality, something which the other
Western nations are only now, in their own terms, en-
countering, but toward which the Italians have managed
— with risk — to maintain a certain superb indifference.
The British government to this day is in important respects oligarchical (until 1918 still placing a property
qualification on the male franchise). The American federal government was conceived in terms of an agrarian
(and slaveholding) society, a yeoman citizenry, a "nat-

It might be possible to compel them by force to *say* that they are free,
but not to compel them by force to *be*, that is to say, to *feel* free. . . .
[With the French Revolution] and the metaphysical adventure which it
started, a new torment came to afflict humanity."

ural" governing aristocracy of accomplishment and service.

The modern liberal state has really been created in the years since 1914. Just as the campaigns of the World War opened with lancers and uhlans skirmishing according to the mounted tactics of the Franco-Prussian War, and the French infantry wore red pantaloons, despised prudence and was devoted to a disastrous doctrine of unprepared assault and use of the bayonet (willfully indifferent to the industrialization of war, the implications of the trenches, barbed wire, and rapid-fire weapons employed in the American Civil War and the Russo-Japanese War), so the political societies of Europe entered World War I resembling the dynastic regimes of the eighteenth century far more than modern mass democracies.

Between 1914 and 1918 the modern state was inadvertently invented. Societies were disciplined to total struggle and the sacrifice of whole age cohorts, the economies nationalized to the purpose of war production, mass propaganda in the new popular press and indoctrination invented, the elites of society and the professions and arts all subordinated to a titanic struggle over issues which — immediately the war was over — seemed of unbearable unimportance. They had fought over naval and colonial prestige; a "place in the sun" for Germany; the fate of Germany's colonies — Tanganyika, Ruanda-Urundi, the desert waste of South-West Africa. The real outcome was thirty million casualties and a fateful metamorphosis in the character of Western political society.

And the transformation of Russia. In Western Europe's invention of the Moloch society-at-war, the Bolsheviks discovered political and social techniques which they institutionalized in order to bring about a revolutionary mobilization of old Russia. Much in what we have come to understand as "totalitarian" society was evolved in conditions of emergency, foreign intervention, civil war — and ignorance — by the desperate Bolshevik elite. They found themselves in possession of an archaic and impoverished state; they possessed only a naïve and unworkable governmental doctrine of simple and spontaneous self-rule by a liberated proletariat (which, in any event, did not exist in important numbers in Russia, a nation of serfs), and they improvised according to the model at hand, which happened to be the model of the Western liberal war state. Thus they launched "war Communism," with "campaigns" and "battles" on the "heavy industrial front" or the "agricultural sector," creating heroes of labor, killing or imprisoning masses of domestic enemies — "class enemies" — slackers, dissidents, "middle peasants," bourgeois.

The Soviet experience — war *à outrance* against the old nature of European society — was to exercise a fascination over the disillusioned intellectuals and restless young people of the West's middle classes as the postwar years brought inflation, unemployment and the return to power of the "old gang." It attracted the unsettled ranks of Western industrial workers, but also, perversely, the newer right-wing revolutionary improvisers (they can hardly be called ideologues) who invented the Fascism of the 1930's — that dramatic mixture of romantic nationalism, militarism, the redemptive military fraternalism of the war years, and — as the contemporary phrase asserted — "Brown Bolshevism."

The Bolsheviks and Fascists together made up a powerful if incoherent force of illiberalism by the 1930's, and their influence was not spent when by 1945 they had worked through their *folie à deux* and all but slaughtered one another — as well as a score of other national victims. The Soviet example — its perfection of the techniques of political warfare, its world-revolutionary rhetoric, its savage tactics while incorporating postwar Eastern Europe — then affected the United States as it, in turn, was drawn into combat. The United States emerged from the early Cold War with Stalinist Russia in some important degree ideologized and disciplined to unending combat, to "struggle for the world."

The influence of totalitarian revolution and millennial ideology still is not spent. The combination of Stalinism's apparent threat to the West in the late 1940's and the institutional models which totalitarian government provided gave rise to, among other modern institutions, the present-day apparatus of Western intelligence and security services which would have been wholly inconceivable to prewar America, and inconceivable in their present dimensions and influence to prewar Europe.* Today, in the United States at least, the intelligence service is acknowledged to be richer, brainier and more influential than the cabinet department constitutionally responsible for foreign policy, and in addition it controls, or influences on decisive issues, an immense range of organizations and organs of public opinion abroad, and even within the United States. The CIA, in its present size and power, might be regarded as the last and most imposing legacy of that revolutionary idealist Leon Trotsky, advocate of unremitting international class struggle, and of the Comintern of the 1920's and 1930's, the organi-

* Even the celebrated — or notorious — British Secret Service was until World War II an underfinanced "amateur" operation according to a wartime recruit, "a mechanism for gathering up the gun-room gossip of Europe."

zation which virtually invented modern propaganda, popular front strategies and political infiltration.

But even before the Bolshevik experience had radiated back into Europe, and Fascism had confirmed the genocidal potentialities of totalitarian government, the Western liberal states had found it impossible to demobilize. Before 1914 — as the memoirs of the survivors bitterly recount —Europe was a world without passports (and without income tax), where the passenger railroads were elegant and efficient, diplomacy and the higher reaches of civil service occupations for gentlemen. It was a world (except for Germany) largely without social services, helpless — even self-congratulatorily so, in the Calvinist moral and Benthamite economic traditions — before the cycles of economy and trade. It was a world where a European agricultural laborer was paid in pennies and kind; where his wife and children gleaned the harvested fields for their own winter stores; where illiterate boys began work at twelve, and if they were strong and ambitious joined the army in order to send home more money than their fathers could earn. In the army, they found food and health; and practiced a matter-of-fact sodomy, while their officers elegantly perpetuated in their messes the archaic aristocratic traditions of the officer corps of Wellington and Frederick the Great. After 1918 it was a different civilization.

It was a modern civilization. The institutions of government and society were transformed, but within a static framework of nineteenth-century parliaments, the husk of traditional privilege, a traditional party system representing class, parochial (communal) and regional interests. There were in Europe parties for the Protestant, the Catholic and the Freemason, for the small entrepreneur, the member of the *haute bourgeoisie*, the aristocrat and the peasant. The new Communist and Fascist parties burst this framework; they were unassimilable in such a system. That they consciously made a revolutionary repudiation of the system itself was only dimly and angrily grasped and the implications of that repudiation not at all, at least not until the 1940's.

I I

The liberal political system had originally been created for societies smaller than ours, homogeneous, largely isolated, restricted in their external power, ruled in fact if not in name by elites of property owners, agrarian landlords and yeoman farmers. Today, in vast contrast, these eighteenth- and nineteenth-century mechanisms of representative government have come to grapple with issues of huge scale and complexity, directly affecting the daily lives — and bearing the burden of the deaths — of millions. That our political system has not been exploded by all of this is remarkable enough. Actually it has been improvised upon, overhauled, added to: vast bureaucracies have been created and authority delegated to special commissions, experts and interest groups. The liberal governmental system has sought to maintain itself by relying on personality and techniques of mass persuasion and publicity, and in its effort to remain responsive to the public, has increasingly turned to mass communications and an informal opinion-sampling process which of its nature seeks irresponsible opinion (in contrast to the act of voting, which is responsible, since it is a formal act with a definite outcome).

The liberal economy has gone through an even more extraordinary series of changes, through laissez faire to

CARNEGIE LIBRARY
LIVINGSTONE COLLEGE
SALISBURY, N. C. 28144

Keynesianism, to international financial management, to varieties of mixed socialist and free-market arrangements, to governmental subsidy as well as effective governmental control of great sectors of the economy, to a situation today where government itself has, throughout the West, become the principal consumer of the technologically most advanced sectors of the economy — and regards the well-being of that sector as a national interest. In industry as a whole a process is under way analogous to that which has already occurred in agriculture in the Western countries: producing the necessities of life occupies a smaller and smaller part of the economy, while services, and a "quaternary" sector (to use Herman Kahn's and Anthony Wiener's phrase) of services to the service sector, grow larger. Production is increasingly of luxuries — which are not to be despised — but also of trivialities for which demand must be stimulated and which pose important questions of social value and purpose. The power of the property-owning class has been obscured, diminished, by the broadening of securities ownership and the "managerial revolution," but now the social power of managers is in turn diminished by the influence — formal but also indirect and often uncalculated — of the state and of a "technostructure" of theoreticians, state managers and state-financed experts, all with loyalties and priorities which lie outside the marketplace itself, and to an important extent even lie outside the formal apparatus of governmental decision and policy.

In a blunt and generalized way the political process today can set certain basic priorities of the economy. It can buy war goods, highways or hospitals. It can subsidize housing or transport construction. But the inner dynamics of the business and industrial system can also influence if not determine the real consequences of those decisions, and since that inner dynamism is directed to profits for management and job security for the workers, and is deeply interrelated with the state bureaucracy and the political process, the government often finds itself as much the prisoner of the economy as its director. The military sector of the American economy more than any other is the client of government; but the government is also the client of defense industry, as its difficulties in controlling even the costs and quality of its military purchases reveal — and this is to say nothing of the troubles which ensue from an attempt to make a basic investment transfer to other economic sectors. This is no simple matter of privilege, lobbies and political pressures, but as recent events have shown, of condemning companies to bankruptcy, disbanding organizations which possess unique technical abilities, experience, staffs and work forces (63 percent of all American scientists, engineers and technicians are employed in defense projects), causing drastic repercussions all down the line of suppliers and subcontractors, throwing into uncertainty the largest single sector of the American productive plant.

In short, the workings and priorities of the modern liberal economies seem to fall more into a regime of necessity than a regime of political choice. Moreover, the incoherence of our understanding and sense of objectives further obscures even what social choices might be made.

For the individual citizen, his relationship to the liberal economy involves very much an act of faith (or of submission), derived from impotence. He is unable to do very much about the economy, even through the political apparatus. But he also is unable to know even what might be done. The situation is at the same time deeply influenced by the experience over a quarter century of general prosperity and economic progress in the liberal West. For the generations under middle age there has been a popular experience of economic success and a demonstration of general competence on the part of the political, financial and private managers of the economy. What will happen if this success crumbles? Perhaps the greatest single threat which still hangs over liberal society today is that the trade imbalances, growing protectionism and liquidity crisis in the 1970's will provoke a major international economic crisis. If that should happen, as seems perfectly likely, what we today describe as a crisis of liberal confidence, of the legitimacy of liberal government, can become a collapse.

In the 1920's and 1930's there was a fundamental difference between the great European and American economic crises. In the United States the system of government seems never to have been seriously threatened. Even the big American socialist movement (which polled 6 percent of the presidential vote in 1912, and by World War I held seventy-nine mayors' offices and had placed a representative in Congress) functioned within the liberal system and became wrecked only in the 1920's when its militant factions, emulating Russia, demanded a revolutionary program. The radical left failed when the Stalinists insisted on imposing an analysis of American reality which the common sense of the workers saw to be irrelevant. America was not Romanov Russia or even Weimar Germany. The American populism of the Depression years reflected a stubborn confidence in the possibilities of the American system ("Every man a king!" was Huey Long's promise) rather than any radical repudiation of it. The popular economic panaceas born of the Depression (the

Townsend Plan, Upton Sinclair's scheme to "share the wealth") revealed a dotty but characteristically American optimism. Except among urban intellectuals* the mood still was not revolutionary — not even among the Okies, migrating to California, or the steel and auto workers being harassed by state troopers and Harry Bennett's Ford Motor Company special police. The labor violence of the 1930's, often described as worse than today's ghetto and student violence, was directed to getting labor into "the system," not to destroying it. The CIO dominated the labor activists — not the IWW or the Communist cells. Franklin Roosevelt, by demonstrating a determination to master the Depression and make the system work, easily swung the mass of Americans to his support.

But in Europe in the same period there was nothing like this shaken but unbroken confidence in the potentialities of the liberal political and economic system. The European system of government had in 1914 insouciantly created a war it could not end before some ten million men had been killed, Russia and Germany were plunged into revolutionary chaos, and the British and French empires fatally weakened — an era of European world dominance politically and militarily undermined and morally discredited. It then failed to cope with inflation and depression; its leading classes proved largely incompetent and often corrupt. For Europe, the Fascist and Bolshevik appeals to "cleanse the world" seemed reasonable enough. Yet liberal politics and economics, at horrendous cost, did ultimately survive even that crisis.

* Rexford Tugwell remarked in 1932: "No one can live and work in New York this winter without a profound sense of uneasiness." But revolution? Elmer Davis says that question, even among the intellectuals, was raised "apathetically, as if nothing they might do could either help or hinder it."

Today the system again is challenged, strained by intensified versions of those same new forces of ferocious change and social dissolution which made up the volatile social mixture from which the first Western crisis exploded. The allegedly "revolutionary" issues of the present day — black rebellion and urban poverty in America, university crises and student rebellion throughout the West, breakdown of urban services and government, bureaucratic atrophy, maldirected economic priorities — nearly all are merely symptoms of strain and structural incompetence. The truly dangerous crisis is moral.

There no longer is unqualified confidence in the legitimacy — which is to say, the right and competence to rule — of liberal government. This must be called a moral crisis because there is no certain evidence that the practical and functional problems of Western society — this most empirical and rationalist of societies — could not in themselves be eventually resolved or reduced. A moral crisis arises not when problems seem very great, but when there no longer is a secure belief that we *deserve* to resolve them: that we have a *right* to go on in this way.

I I I

The essential liberal faith is in the marketplace: in the beneficent outcome of the free play of ideas and popular forces. Liberalism assumes the power and ultimate success of reasoned action. Today this faith is in doubt, like the Christian's act of faith in the existence of the Deity. The analogy suggests something more. Christianity in modern times has reconciled itself to doubt; it survives on philosophically existential terms. Its conditions of survival have become Pascal's, an existential gamble, and this in fact may be the only possible outcome of our crisis of secular doubt. Reason, too, no longer is able to rely upon material proofs for validation. The material results of reason are in popular doubt. For medieval man, miracles provided popular proof of God's existence and benevolent intervention in human affairs. The marketplace has been the modern arena of faith in the miraculous benevolence of ineffable forces. A faith that the free play of market forces will eventually end in Good is, in fact, more "absurd" than religious belief, for there, at least, there is a presumption of an intelligent Agent Who writes straight with His crooked lines. Reason in our time, then, has to be defended as something of self-contained value, immanent value, an activity *appropriate to man,* an activity which no longer can arrogantly make absolute claims but only provisional ones, diffidently justified as the best of bad choices in a universe of bad choices.

But the rational faith today has cracked, most of all among the intelligentsia. The primacy of intention, affect, feeling, is asserted by important Western elites. Reason is attacked as a factor of dehumanization, the diminishment of life. It is held that reason itself — in the agency of expert government, the work of technological, economic and political specialists — has come to produce a mad disordering of the world and of the human relationship to the material universe. Reason acting through science, and its offspring technology, has come to seem a juggernaut of disruption, uncontrollable and indiscriminate, indifferently wrecking at the same time that it creates.

These are the views of many Western intellectuals, members of the elites; and this itself is an important evidence of crisis. But beyond the alienation of intellectuals and elites is a significant popular alienation. Its immediate causes lie in a series of practical or structural failures in Western political society, which may yet become compounded by equivalent blunders of economic management. But the critical shock, the catalytic agent of the crisis of liberal legitimacy, has been supplied in international relations. A moral intelligibility has been lost in the militant relationship of the Western liberal nations, self-consciously led by the United States, with the rest of the world.

I say this is critical because foreign affairs provide the dramatic modern frame for coherent communal action, for national self-definition and self-identification. Increasingly, international politics have provided a stage for moral action — or for morality's counterfeit, ideological action. In the last fifty years — since Woodrow Wilson, to take the obvious time frame, although Wilson only gave a crucial articulation to more complex developments in international and American politics — individual identity in the Western nations has become deeply bound up in national identity and action. One reason for this is that the national community is nearly the only moral community which survives for our socially mobile, socially adrift Western population. Nationalism has become more of a popular force since Wilson's effort to replace it with an internationalist community; it has not faded.

People have lost their sense of distance, that insulation which once existed between individual men and national and international crises; the result has been an individual involvement — a private, emotional investment — which is unprecedented in intensity. At the same time men have come to feel themselves committed, or threatened, in quite new ways by what happens in the world. They are constantly told to intensify their political involvement. They

58

are told that their responsibility is greater than ever before, that the political actions and decisions of the individual citizen are of unprecedented importance, that the fate of the nation, history itself — the fate of the world — ride on their decisions.

Yet the thing which most forcibly strikes the individual citizen is, of course, how little power he has. Less than ever before, it seems, can he really affect what happens. His personal involvement and responsibility seem huge; at the same time he feels powerless to change anything. Not only is the individual's vote one among millions, but many of the old channels by which he could influence government and communicate with his leaders have broken down. The issues themselves seem so complex and the forces so impersonal that the individual doubts that he can even understand what should be done. He cannot feel convinced that his congressman or his deputy in Parliament really has a crucial role in the great decisions made by government. There has been a "postparliamentary" trend in modern liberal government, enhancing executive authority at the expense of parliaments and the lower levels of legislative and party debate. The role of political opposition even at the highest levels is often drastically reduced through coalition government or the fragmentation of opposition among weak parties, themselves hostile to one another. Thus the individual often is denied detailed representation on issues, or even denied the opportunity to commit himself to a politically effective opposition. When NDP, the neo-Fascist party in West Germany, campaigned against the Grand Coalition government of Socialists and Christian Democrats at the end of the 1960's by claiming to provide the only opposition — the only opportunity to say "no" — it was, of course, quite correct.

The result of all this has been stress, anxiety, distraction among individuals, as well as an intensification of domestic political controversy and conflict. People feel impotent in the midst of unimaginable power; and impotence is conducive to hysterical behavior. They search for solutions, for some relief from the tension created within them. When, as it did in the mid-1960's, the American Congress failed to articulate any opposition at all to so grave an issue as the war in Vietnam, and in the same period a third or more of its committee meetings were held in secret; when even the Senate Foreign Relations Committee — in belated criticism of America's Asian policy — is deprived by the Executive of comprehensive information on American operations and commitments in Vietnam, Cambodia, Laos and Thailand, the popular sense of frustration and impotence becomes very significant.

The Vietnam war opposition involves, in America, one political grouping, largely of the left. But conventionally conservative citizens have encountered the same frustrations. The American lower middle class, lately rediscovered by politicians and press, has suffered deep and unheard grievances for more than a decade. Some are practical grievances of economic discrimination and victimization. More are the inchoate grievances which arise from a sense of impotence, of a deaf government. As Michael Novak has remarked, they have come to feel that "somewhere, far away, in 'Washington,' leaders are daily arranging, without consulting them, new ways to intensify the difficulties they face." Novak adds that where the lower middle class once was opposed by landed owners, now it is by an educated managerial elite. "Its older opponents kept its members from control over their destiny by economic privilege; its new opponents keep them from similar control by technical expertise. The old system was plutocratic; the new one is meritocratic. Both leave a very large class feeling increasingly helpless."

The rage of the workingman and the small entrepreneur or craftsman is antielitist, antitechnocratic, anti-intellectual, and to a considerable degree antimodern. The "modern" developments in government and society provide a nexus for resentments which go far beyond the specific and remediable grievances which the workingman experiences. His reaction veers toward that of the anomic petit-bourgeois Nazi of the 1930's anxious to be rid in one blow of socialism, plutocracy, pornography, newspapers, the Versailles Treaty and jazz music. His reaction is akin to that of the French *Poujadist* of the mid-1950's who belonged to a political movement directed against an anonymous "higher authority" perceived as manifestly unresponsive to the wishes of the people. *Poujadism* began among small shopkeepers, and thus it identified the source of France's ills as "international finance," "vagabond capital," "stateless" banks and trusts. It resisted a centralizing, rationalizing, economic process which in France of the mid-1950's was undermining the role of private shopkeepers and provincial businessmen. But the enemy was seen in much larger terms: as modern liberal government itself, dominated by "elitists" and supported by those intellectuals whose function it is "to befuddle and confuse the French people." This might as well be Spiro Agnew speaking of American liberal intellectuals and television commentators, or Governor George Wallace's rather more vivid rhetoric of "pointy-headed professors" who control the "liberal establishment" in Washington. And Mr. Wallace, of course, would not exclude the Nixon Administration — which has its own corps of professors — from his strictures.

The Nixon Administration, in search of a constituency and beleaguered by war critics, fell upon the "middle American" in 1970, not so much because his social and economic demands coincided with what the Administration wanted to accomplish (they did not; the interests of the blue-collar worker are not those of the provincial business executive or upper-middle-class entrepreneur who traditionally supplies the Republican party's leadership and defines its platforms), but because the "middle American" was a patriot and nationalist. The distress of this "middle American" over the New Left's antipatriotic symbols and rhetoric, his anger at the obscenity and self-conscious defiance of conventional morality of the student movement, created in America of the 1970's a provisional alliance of Administration and white workingmen against the New Left and its real and supposed allies. I say that this was a provisional alliance because there is no true congruence of interest or belief on the war issue — as an Administration failure to end the war will inevitably demonstrate.

As with so much else in the Vietnam controversy, there has been a deep obscuring of real popular attitudes. The desire of the "middle American" to have a "honorable" settlement of the Vietnam war, and his hostility to the student demonstrators, draft-card burning and New Left adulation of the Vietcong, is not at all the same thing as a firm belief in the validity of the war and the necessity for military victory. Indeed, polls typically have consistently reported the highest support for the war — as with other policies of the Administration in power — from among the

American college-graduate population and those with incomes of over $10,000 per year. Manual workers express stronger support for either immediate or gradual withdrawal from the war than white-collar workers or executives and professionals. Studies of the voting pattern in those American communities which have held referendums on the war indicate that the antiwar vote has nearly always been significantly higher in working-class areas than in upper-middle-class districts. One reason for this is perfectly obvious: the sons of workingmen and of the poor are much more likely to serve in combat units than middle-class young men or the college-educated. As Stewart Alsop has bitterly observed, the American draft system, in its class and economic bias, has proved "rotten and corrupt." In 1969 only 10 percent of those drafted were college men, yet college men made up 40 percent of the college-age young. The young workingman has served his country with sacrifices drastically out of proportion to those of the society as a whole.

Those in the Nixon Administration who concluded that the workingman and his family demanded a military victory in Vietnam to justify their sacrifices made an arguable but unproven case — unproven, like so many other assessments of public opinion on this war, because it begged the real possibilities. "Victory," or a version of victory in a war, is clearly an objective to which the vast majority of any national public, and not only the white working classes, will ordinarily give support. But the unasked question remains: Victory at what cost? The cost thus far, for American working families, has been inordinately and unjustly high. The attempt to polarize "middle American" opinion in support of an uncompromising policy has contended that anything less than a recognizable victory (leaving a militantly anti-Communist government in power in South Vietnam) would produce "backlash" and a mood of political repression in America. This inaugurated a process of self-fulfilling prophecy and significantly contributed to bringing about such a "backlash" — and at the same time it added to that popular sense of governmental indifference or inaccessibility to popular feeling, which already was the most imposing new characteristic of American political society.

I V

For it has been a mark of the decade in America that elected officials have found themselves at odds with popular demands. They have themselves become victims of the policy inheritances of their Administrations and the commitments and momentum of the federal government's bureaucracy. It was not, surely, the wish of Lyndon Johnson, elected as a peace candidate, or of Richard Nixon, elected on a platform of ending the Vietnamese war, to find themselves a year after inauguration prosecuting or prolonging an unpopular war. They inherited things done, programs under way, commitments made, a body of official assumptions, all of which combined eventually to pit them against elements in their own constituencies and set them against popular demands which they came to believe irreconcilable with the national interest. The effect of this has been to sharply affect public belief in the accountability of government. For many American voters, their experience in the presidential elections of 1964 and 1968 has contributed to a conviction that voting has been futile and that, in this respect at least, national policy is

irreversible by the established methods of ballot and pe-
tition.

Distrust of established liberal government thus exists
today on both sides of the conventional political barrier,
on both sides of the war debate in America, yet gives voice
to certain common protests and anxieties. There is not
only a New Left and a "New Politics" but a New Populism.
They all attack the "liberal establishment," the elites of
experts and technocrats — those "power elites" who appear in other guises as "effete intellectuals" and the men
who never met a payroll. We know that there was a significant overlap in 1968 between the populist constituency
of Governor Wallace and the New Politics constituency
of Senator Kennedy. The genius of Robert Kennedy was
to respond with vividness and vivacity to people who believed themselves hopelessly remote from power. Eugene
McCarthy's campaign was to "give government back to
the people." It is not just the populists who claim to be unheard; the dominant theme of protest from the left is the
same. There is an ugly agreement that the government is
unresponsive to popular will, arbitrary in its decisions and
actions, ruled by inner circles of bankers or industrialists
or technocrats or generals or intelligence specialists or professors who cannot directly be brought to account and
whose collective power overrides that of the elected officials who do remain subject to recall.

And despite the terminology of this kind of discussion
— that of economic and social classes — it seems clear
that neither the protest of the left or right really expresses
economic or class interest as such. The New Populist is
closer to a traditional classification, but his movement is
essentially ideological, incorporating provincial bankers

and industrialists as well as Alabama wool-hat farmers and unprecedentedly well-paid and secure auto unionists and construction-trades workers. Nor do the urban and suburban middle classes, the established or semiestablished intelligentsia of the "New Politics" movement who are today alienated from "the system," have a common material or class interest. They are the beneficiaries of the system. Nor, black militants excluded, is the New Left a class or interest movement, talk of a student proletariat notwithstanding.

It is new in the American experience that a left-wing radical movement exists which opposes liberal politics and is not drawn from a single class or a marginal element in the population, but in considerable degree derives from the nation's middle classes and elite institutions. It is new that such a movement should impose so wide a claim upon the imagination of a much bigger part of the society, so that revolution is connived at in the best circles. At the same time a second, larger — and more familiar — radical mood develops on the right, and although it is nominally committed to defense of the American system, it too is capable of violence, hostile to the libertarian principle. Both movements would do away with universal tolerance, withdrawing tolerance — in Herbert Marcuse's words — "from regressive [substitute *subversive*] movements before they can become active." Both would evade the conservative constraints of history, denying that we must be imprisoned by past or present, insisting that some vital leap of political action can bring us to a transformed society, rid of anxiety. The truth is that both are ethical movements, directed to no pragmatic change or institutional reform or policy redirection, but to achieving a new moral condition for America.

What the New Left, the New Politics, and the New Populism constitute are not interest groups but alliances of people of different and often divergent interests but with a common sense of outraged values. They are moral and ideological alliances based on discontent with things as they are, a discontent which remains incoherently articulated but has, I believe, a common source. While these groups wage a combat along a conventional left/right barrier on nearly all the positive issues of national policy, the moral anxieties they express — of "lost" American integrity, lost American stature, lost possibilities and national potentialities — articulate in different accents things very much alike. They say that as a practical matter government does not seem to work as it should. But they are also saying that their view of what the national society, the national identity, has become, or should be, no longer is that of the government. And in this profound, indeed anguished, protest of theirs, events in international politics have provided the decisive issues.

CHAPTER IV

The International Crisis

Fifty years ago we Americans substituted melodrama for tragedy, violence for dignity under suffering.

— F. Scott Fitzgerald

Words carry us forward towards ideological confrontations from which there is no retreat. This is the root tragedy of politics. . . . Political conduct is no longer spontaneous or responsive to reality. It freezes around a core of dead rhetoric.

— George Steiner

I

FOR INTERNATIONAL
politics, the Vietnam war has constituted the most san-
guinarily destabilizing event since Hitler marched into
the Rhineland. By that action in 1936 the postwar system
— the Versailles system — was shattered, with eventual
consequences which hardly any contemporary was willing
to contemplate. The Vietnam war once again has discredited a system — of alliances, but more than that, a
moral alignment, a moral order — underpinning the international political structure established in and after
World War II. We are left with a profoundly uncertain
future, but one in which the moral simplicities of the
1950's, and the moral self-confidence of the United States,
seem dreamlike antiquities, memories of a classic age.

For the United States itself, Vietnam has been a moral
catastrophe of a dimension unprecedented in the country's history. It has constituted the calamitous triumph of
American hypocrisy and cant over American seriousness.
It has amounted to an American intellectual act of default
before the realities and possibilities of the political world.
Its effect, within America, has been to catalyze that violence provisionally overcome in the national past, cracking the fragile national vessel, turning an inevitable experience of stress — derived from forces of social dislocation and modern institutional strain — into a frenzy of
national self-laceration and self-defeat.

The abiding America of ambiguously open possibilities

and contingent commitments, where anything could happen and nothing lasts, and every man has a chance and will to move along, and likes to keep a gun in the house, thus was transformed into an America of warring factions, broken heads, vituperation, and fantasied revolutions and counterrevolutions: an America of plots to kill blacks, lock up intellectuals, cancel elections, draw up lists of victims. We exported our own discreditable fears onto Vietnam — fears of world-wide insurrections, race wars, "rural" peoples' assaults upon the "cities" of the liberal industrial West, vast struggles for the world, fears at which our political leaders and academic men had connived. That was bad enough, for we thus licensed ourselves to kill wholesale in the service of cant. Now we have reimported these fantasies, to which our fears gave monstrous life. Inaugurating violence abroad, we have loosed it at home. Exporting counterrevolution, we have imported "revolution." The rhetoric and categories of foreign revolution are displaced onto our domestic society, with students and black militants now declaring themselves "Third World revolutionaries" and our police forces and national guardsmen dealing with them in a fantasy that they are enemy assault infantry, while high officials describe the young — as they have chosen to be described — as alien enemies within. Yet they are all poor bloody Americans, Huey P. Newton and John Mitchell alike.

The extremities of violence to which we resorted undermined our own sense of proportion, of reasonable limit. Our national style of war is indiscriminate, reflecting an unresolved Puritan moral inheritance: all war is wholly evil; some wars are necessary; once we have entered a necessary war, no moral discrimination among the actions of war can be reasonable. On the whole the country believed this, but with a measure of unease as the peasant enemy endured the blows of B-52 raids and our wholesale relocation of district populations and our eradication of forests and farmland and blighting of the very order of nature on the Vietnamese peninsula.

The moral unease produced by *how* we were waging the war proved more devastating than American doubts about *what* we were doing. Americans acted with a bad conscience that revealed itself in the dissimulation of officials, their secrecy, their bribing of allies, and by the early emergence of a domestic opposition which was less political than it was moral — often notably unpolitical, desperately reiterating a supposedly abandoned American moral utopianism. The corruption of official language, the loss of all candor in describing the war, the struggle which broke out between government and the press, reflected this unease: the most violent of the hawks insisted that America "get it over with"; the most principled of them expressed a persistent disquiet at our connivance with terrorism, or our undiscriminating weaponry, our "free fire zones" and unaimed "harassment and interdiction" fire into the countryside.

The meaning of this was that Americans were ashamed of what they and their country was doing, a wholly novel experience in a national society without cynicism about itself. Here lie the roots of the "value crisis" felt so keenly within America as the war progressed. As Stephen Marcus was to remark, even the new pornography emerging in American popular entertainment and art could be understood as "a form of pseudo-radicalism" tied to this sense of loss in the moral authority of the formal structure of society. The display of the American flag on millions of automobiles and homes, its desecration by war opponents, was a symptom of national ambivalence: the defense, exaltation, of the flag was meant to still the doubts not simply of the proclaimed doubters but of those who denied all doubt. There was no longer any *assurance* about being an American. There was no longer moral confidence.

This country had never had anything bad happen to it since the War Between the States. Now it happened, and the nation began to come apart under the strain. Yet it must be said that America was only going — wherever it's going — in a whirl of resistance. The worst still does not have to happen. But the best that can happen is probably bad enough: an age of American sterility, an age of wounded and sullen recovery from this revenge which history is imposing upon us for our sentimentality and our cowardice. Cowardice because we entered Vietnam, as we ourselves dimly grasped, to fight Vietnamese as surrogates, proxies, for another enemy — China, Russia, world Communism? — which we were unable or unwilling to confront, lacking the conviction even of our fantasy. At the same time that we blasted and bombarded Vietnam and Laos in order to overcome Communism, we connived at the Soviet suppression of Czechoslovak liberalism in 1968, sought from the Soviet leaders an agreed "stabilization" in arms and international policy, dealt with circumspection toward nuclear China.

A fear of Russia which was justifiable in the 1940's, a fear of China which had some plausibility in the time of Stalin's savage primacy among Communist party leaders, a sense of world struggle between exclusive alternatives of liberalism and totalitarianism derived from the 1930's and 1940's, had become detached from real reference by the 1960's. They had become a structure of illusions served by a vast apparatus of American foreign and military agencies; and our fear was more dramatic, more palpable, because it no longer was constrained by real reference. So we launched our revenge upon the available and vulnerable Vietnamese Communists.

Not that the Vietcong was not real enough, more real even than our official rhetoric could accommodate. But the threat of the Vietcong was to their fellow Vietnamese. We redefined them to conform to our own global preoccupations, just as we attempted to remake the war itself into that modern clash of ideologies, of air forces and industrialized armies, which we were prepared to fight, a war appropriate to our political and military forces, our national style.

I I

We turned the war into one *suitable* to us; yet it incorrigibly retained its own dimensions, its own Vietnamese perfections, its deviousness, its smallness, its personalized terrors, its private tragedy, leaving us ultimate irrelevancies; and in the end victims of ourselves. We and the Vietnamese Communists hardly had a common grasp of what the war was about. When the United States fought Hitler or the Japanese empire or the Kaiser's Germany, we and they both understood the terms of the conflict and what it would take to bring the war to an end. Victory and defeat were both recognizable, definable. But in Vietnam we and the Vietnamese have often enough claimed victory in the same battles, success in the same political engagements, and this has not been simply a matter of lies or propaganda. There actually have been victories for both sides in the same event, since the two sides were fighting different wars, with contradictory values and expectations. We and they have hardly understood one another when each spoke of war, revolution, liberation, peace, the future.

Ours has been a strategy of the strong, employing technology, fire power and wealth, ostensibly to achieve in Vietnam impersonal objectives: the abstractions of democracy, the containment of Communism, a "free Asia." We believed that the enemy could be forced to make the "reasonable" decisions to compromise or capitulate as choices preferable to the pain, destruction and death we could inflict upon him. Our strategy assumed that if these evils — these "costs" — were implacably imposed upon the Vietcong and the North Vietnamese, at some point in the process the issues of the war would come to seem less valuable to them than to stop the suffering and destruction. Ours has been a reasonable strategy, perfected within a community of political scientists and technologists who scrupulously abjured passion, rhetoric and real feeling, the ungeneralizable data of real life; but it was of course the strategy of those who are rich, who love life and fear "costs."

Theirs has been the strategy of the weak, practicing defiant and personalized violence, stoically accepting the destruction of wealth and the loss of lives. The weak deal in absolutes, among them that man inevitably suffers and dies. When the weak are confronted with the alternatives of death or capitulation, the one may be as plausible a choice as the other. Interrogations of Vietcong prisoners, when they were asked what would happen if the Americans did not give up the war and quit the country, often have elicited such uncomprehending replies as that "then we will all die."

For the strong, it may be a reasonable choice to surrender in a given situation. To die for a cause may be necessary on occasion, or noble, but we see it as the outcome of an unreasonable situation. We want life, happiness, wealth, power, and we assume that in a reasonable society all these are possible. But happiness, wealth, power — the very words in conjunction reveal a dimension of our experience beyond that of the Asian poor. For us, then, death and suffering are irrational choices when alternatives exist. For the weak, there may be no intelligible choice.

The strategy of the weak is a conscious strategy of idealists and ideologues. It turns the strength of an Asian peasantry — its capacity for endurance in suffering — against the vulnerability of the strong. It does this by inviting the strong to carry their own strategic logic to its conclusion, which is genocide. (The Chinese Communists seem to have said this explicitly, although it is not clear that they understand the significance of the claim which Mao Tse-tung has made that China can "win" a nuclear war in which 300 million Chinese would die.)

The strategy of the weak is to force us, the strong, to do what is most abhorrent to us, to carry out these threats which reveal our own priorities of value. In projecting our own values onto Asians, we assume that the threat of punishment and destruction is the ultimate threat, inevitably forcing a "reasonable" settlement of the war. When they defy us we find ourselves asked to carry out the threat — and we balk. They are inviting us to do what we ourselves most fear. And we grasp obscurely that to do it is to destroy ourselves — that by contradicting our own value system we destroy it. Thus we have drawn back from all that we might have done against North Vietnam: from nuclear weapons, eventually even from the bombing of North Vietnam, which was accomplishing little. We officially reversed ourselves under Richard Nixon, but without courage — with a willfully contradictory argument that what the Vietnamese Communists would not yield under the force of bombardment and the threat of escalation, they would yield under the threat of our withdrawal from Vietnam. Or so it seemed; yet the change merely revealed our own sense of the futility of what we had been doing and at the same time our lack of the integrity to admit the logic of what we wanted to do. To quit Vietnam now would be to accept that we had been defeated there. We have not the courage for that; yet Vietnam does not release us. We can no more escape the problem through "Vietnamization" and withdrawal than we could bomb it away. The crisis will come, at some point in the early 1970's, when again we will confront the dreaded alternatives of our own defeat — or South Vietnam's collapse — or administering new destruction upon Vietnam, and upon our own convictions of identity and value as well.

We are, one supposes, ultimately capable of either action: ignoring defeat or launching an even worse new war. American foreign policy has always been an unreal mixture of idealism and Puritanism, and the Puritan side has in the past had a Cromwellian dimension to it of killing for the Lord, denying human value to the national enemy, exterminating him at the antiseptic distance which technology makes possible. We have also in this war learned something of the new moral dimensions of ideological war, of deliberate terrorism, assassination, political reprisals, murder *pour encourager les autres*, the "generation" of refugees, rendering a landscape uninhabitable.

But there are moral frontiers which we may yet cross in Vietnam.

I I I

It is the contradiction between our idealism and our Puritanism which has so disrupted the American nation as Vietnam has worn on. The war began with the two adjoined: when John Kennedy ordered Special Forces to Vietnam, when Dwight Eisenhower before him had made the first American commitments to Ngo Dinh Diem and to the creation of a liberal "Third Force" in Vietnam (as against the Communists on the one side and the colonial French and their Vietnamese favorites on the other), even when Lyndon Johnson began the bombing of the North, Americans could still convince themselves that this was a struggle consistent with the struggles against totalitarianism of the 1950's and the 1940's. But it was not that at all, and this has steadily come to be understood — even in the very act of denial and emotional repression.

The great and enduring political damage of this war will be for that American liberal internationalism which launched it — and for the Democratic party liberals who began it and the Republican internationalists who continue to prosecute it. This is, one must understand, the liberals' war, which is to say that it is the misshapen outgrowth of a series of assumptions about politics and history which have been at the heart of that liberal internationalism which has been animating the American political consciousness since Woodrow Wilson.

America entered the Vietnam war believing that it wanted for the Vietnamese only what the Vietnamese would—or should—want for themselves. This conviction was consistent with the much more extensive claim made upon the world by the modern American political imagination that there is a fundamental identity of political aspiration and value between Americans and all men everywhere.* When Secretary of State Dean Rusk, in the early months of the Vietnam war, declared that America's goals are those "of a great majority of mankind; this identity of basic purpose gives us friend and allies in many nations," he was merely providing a fatuous echo to the old Wilsonian conviction (to quote Woodrow Wil-

* Elsewhere Edmund Stillman and I have discussed at length the sources and implications of this American view of the national relationship to the world abroad (in *Power and Impotence* [1966] and *The New Politics* [1961]). The point has recently been taken up in New Left analyses of American policy, hardening our criticism and usually attributing the American effort to impose characteristically American structures and solutions upon other societies to the actions of a single privileged class (an Establishment) or to economic motives, an economically determined "neo-imperialism." This neo-Marxist case, made most intelligently by Gabriel Kolko in his *The Politics of War* and *The Roots of American Foreign Policy*, seems to me fundamentally mistaken. It is no news to argue that America is a capitalist society with a commitment to free trade and a hostility to socialist economics, but America's "neo-imperialism" has expressed American popular conviction, conceived in idealistic terms, far more than the selfish interests of any economic elite; and the Vietnam war itself cannot reasonably be understood in these categories of economic interest. Indeed, Vietnam has all but wrecked America's trade balances and international liquidity, provoking serious domestic inflation, precipitous stock-market shifts, protectionism, and a crisis of economic confidence which could become a depression. The neo-Marxist interpretation of American foreign policy is procrustian and anachronistic, whatever its merit as an irritant to the conventional wisdom. And too often, as in the work of the brilliant linguist Noam Chomsky (*American Power and the New Mandarins*), it veers into a Manichaean politics of setting on the one side a conspiratorial liberal elite, enemies of the people, and on the other an innocent "popular force." The regrettable truth is that the foreign policy of the United States in the postwar period has, for the most part, been a popular policy, pursued out of Wilsonian motivations and for reformist, even utopian, goals. The criticism to be made of it is that it has become callow, sentimental, savagely stupid in many of its actions, if anything too "popular," too American, too little the work of an intellectually serious leadership, even of an intellectually serious oligarchy — who might at least be expected to understand the conjunction of national interest with their selfish interests and not wreck both.

son as he presented the Versailles agreement to Congress in 1919) that America's is "the flag of all mankind." What Vietnam has accomplished is brutally to teach Americans that this is not so. The lesson has shaken the individual American's sense of his own identity and value. Who is an American *sub specie aeternitatis:* once he was a liberator; and the world confirmed him in believing this. No longer is it so.

Not that the lesson has not already been forced upon a reluctant America. Our postwar struggle with Russia and China during the 1950's and early 1960's involved a set of positive beliefs about how world politics could be reordered, and how the economic success — the "development" — of the advanced states could be transplanted to the preindustrial Third World. Federalism, regional economic and political confederation, was expected to replace the national system of Europe. Later a progressive federation of zones of the Third World would undoubtedly follow. There was a real American popular commitment to the belief that a new and co-operative mode of international relations could be brought into being, rivaling Communism's violent model for revolutionary change. Economic development of the Third World was invested with very large expectations of steady and peaceful progress; growing prosperity was expected in turn to produce political order, and the early political disruptions of the area were taken to be transitional, or the result of deliberate intervention by the Communists.

But just as American confidence in the possibilities of international reform was once very high indeed, today it is very low, with a considerable reversion to old isolationist attitudes. We enjoyed two decades of a fairly altruistic internationalism in the popular attitudes of this country

— reflected, if more skeptically, within Western Europe
— because all the Western nations believed in themselves.
Our institutions worked, our prosperity soared, our internal
controversies were creative, shaping national policies.
Now this confidence no longer exists. Until recent
years there was in the United States none of the self-
doubt which characterized postwar Europe in its deal-
ings with ex-colonial Asia and Africa. Moreover, at least
in the 1940's, and early 1950's, there was a reciprocal Afro-
Asian regard for the United States; we were not widely
regarded among Asian and African elites as having inherited the imperialist role as such. In addition, nuclear
weapons provided the United States with an unprecedented dimension of power, beyond that which it held
as the world's chief industrial nation and the liberator of
Western Europe from Nazism. In the first years after
World War II the United States briefly assumed a role of
unchallenged world primacy. We were the "super"-power.
That now is ended.

The change has meant far more than a vindication of
guerrilla tactics and guerrilla ideologies against regular
military forces. Colonial wars in the past were won by
the colonizer because everyone understood that he was
destined to win. Now the Western "neo-imperialist" no
longer is convinced that he has a right to win. He no
longer is convinced that his is the superior society. The
Vietnam war, its antecedent French Indochina war, the
Algerian war, all have been rationalized as for the sake of
saving their victims from a worse form of foreign exploitation; but increasingly this argument has been pushed to
the side. The reality now is that American elites — and
European — doubt that Western culture, to say nothing
of a Western version of economic "modernization," is of

value to the Third World, or even, it may be, doubt that it is of unalloyed value in itself.

I V

Until 1968 the essential terms of the Cold War had been bipolar conflict, a dynamic competition between the two greatest powers in which the European states and Japan could act to enforce, exploit or mediate the relationship. The rivalry was on fundamental, important issues, moderated by a shared (or militarily induced) recognition of the reasonable limits of competition. Within those limits each side imposed important restraints upon the other's freedom of action. The expression "detente," describing this relationship, meant competitive balance, and was distinguished from "entente."

As recently as the start of the 1960's, it was possible to describe the relationship of the great powers — Russia and America, the major European states and Japan — as involving conflicts of intelligible and vital moral visions of society. As late as in the Khrushchev era, Soviet Russia seemed reopened to change and adaptation, still animated by a workable, if warped, vision of a reform, the creation of a socialist commonwealth released from the arbitrary forms (and modes of mobilization) imposed by Stalin. At that time, even the illiberalism of Soviet society seemed "modern" and positive in quality, which is to say totalitarian, driven by a version of those progressive historicist ideas characteristic of society in the European West. But Khrushchev himself proved to have no real solution for Russia, even though he ended considerable evil, and his successors have increasingly taken on the reactionary role. Unable — and unwilling — to shed the inheritance of Leninism and Stalinism, they are at the same time unable to make it work satisfactorily. They are attacked by the Chinese ideologists for their marginal accommodations to economic reform and for the "great-power politics" they have chosen to play, and at the same time they have lost the ability to command willing allegiance from the elites of Eastern Europe and the nonruling Communist parties of Western Europe and the Third World. The Soviets' international situation reflects the internal dilemma, and the outcome has become a defiant yet unconfident attempt to perpetuate the status quo as the gulf widens between the official ideology, a specific creation of the Russian revolutionary situation between 1917 and 1939, and the contemporary needs of industrial Russia. Certainly analogies with Russia of the first fourteen years of this century are inevitable, with the shocks of 1904-1905 lacking: an obscurantist bureaucracy is kept in power by a reactionary secret police; the literary and artistic intelligentsia is defiant but powerless; the technocratic intelligentsia is restless but unimaginative; the leaders themselves have no clear idea of what to do or where to go, and have fallen back on reiterating the old doctrines they no longer quite believe themselves.

The Cold War was an intelligible American national mission when Soviet Russia was a closed and messianic society, presenting an intelligible challenge. Today certain of the beliefs and institutions of the Cold War coexist with a fairly widely held sense of inevitable alliance with Russia; the Chinese are the new threat to us both. Yet even this — the "dual-condominium" or "convergence" model — was last year's belief, and Mr. Nixon has moved a short distance toward normalization of relations with China.

The malaise of the two superpowers has produced a discernible, although not at all conclusive, movement toward each other in their essential world policies. That is to say, that each, preoccupied with the contradictions of its political and intellectual inheritances, is anxious to avoid changes which could further unsettle them both. In practical terms this has meant preservation of the status quo in Europe, a guarded hostility in the Middle East, a mutual hostility toward China (and a shared, and unrealistically inflated, preoccupation with China as a world power). There has been a "convergence" of Soviet and American systems rather different from that envisaged in the optimistic theories either of American analysts of the mid-1960's or of dissident Soviet scientists at the end of the decade. The key events in this process were the war in Vietnam and the Soviet invasion of Czechoslovakia in 1968. The first destroyed the moral consensus upon which the Western alliance had rested, causing both Western Europe and Japan to regard the United States as, at best, an unwise, unpredictable and unbalancing force in the world. The second blasted widely held expectations about Soviet political liberalization and evolution — and more important, included some degree of American connivance or positive acquiescence in the Soviet move.* The significance of that factor was not lost

---

* Whereas in 1956 the United States had organized and led a campaign of political and economic reprisals against Russia for its invasion of Hungary, in 1968, even though the quality of the Czech reforms was far less provocative to Russia and involved far less risk to Soviet security perceptions and interests, and even though the invasion was widely understood to be a clear possibility sometime in advance and was predicted by some Western analysts, virtually nothing was done by the United States either to deter it or to exact a penalty from Russia for it. Yet the opportunities were much greater than they had been in 1956 simply because Russia was much more deeply involved in trade and political relations with the West and had a good deal more to lose from Western economic reprisals or boycott, a serious suspension or breaking off of

on the European publics, nor was the significance of the nonproliferation treaty's attempt to freeze present nuclear-power relationships.

Now the relationship of the superpowers is changed, and indeed the change may be seen by the world as greater than either the United States or the Soviet Union intends or is prepared to acknowledge. The ideological rivalry obviously persists; we and the Soviets continue to struggle for political influence; we and the Soviet Union have important commitments to regionally competitive states, as in the Middle East; but our hearts are no longer in the struggle. A real change has occurred in the Soviet-American relationship which the Czechoslovak crisis only made explicit. Ours and Russia's nuclear power, our preeminence of power and risk — our shared vulnerability to international crises — give us important interests in common. We share an interest in controlling the dangers and expense of nuclear competition, an interest in preventing the spread of these weapons, an interest in countering those third-party challenges or "uncontrollable" regional conflicts which, from our point of view, must compound the complexities and threats of international affairs. Our relationship is no longer what it was in Stalin's day or even in the Khrushchev era. It is a web of rival and collaborative interests and ambitions; it is a competition whose terms implicitly limit the roles of other

---

arms-control negotiations, a positive (if self-penalizing) resumption by the United States of the arms race and increase in arms budgets. There obviously was no reasonable way for this country actually to prevent the invasion, but the price exacted for it — and the deterrent effect of describing that price ahead of time — could have been made much higher than in 1956. It is difficult to avoid the conclusion that in 1968 American officials were secretly relieved when Russia so efficiently removed this irritant to stable Soviet-American relations. "Munich," in this case, provided a convenient precedent, if one that it seemed better not to dwell upon.

powers. To the extent that the collaborative elements have been recognized in Soviet policy and ours, we and the Soviet Union have become aligned on the same side of what becomes a grossly unbalanced international system.

In this situation, an attempt to restore balance to the international system becomes very likely, probably by a qualified but important European and Japanese political and military reassertion. The passivity of Japan and the West European nations over the last two decades was never, in any event, a condition which could be relied upon to endure, and now a crucial incentive to action has been supplied. The important question is whether Western Europe and Japan possess the will to action, a question to which we must return later in this book. For the present it is necessary to say that they, too, are victims of the inner crisis of liberal society, and the domestic factors and the external act upon one another. Europe's own national vulnerabilities in the new conditions of international society provide a stimulus to European renewal, and at the same time such a renewal could radiate outward upon the international system. World "leadership," unlike world "rule," implies acknowledgment of a nation's — or a group of nations' — fitness to lead.

But today the old spell is broken. The Cold War, which some of us declared a decade ago to be over, now really is finished — in a welter of embitterment and confusion.[*]

---

[*] ". . . we have not won the Cold War, nor lost it, at least as that war was conceived in the beginning. Perhaps the Soviets have not yet begun to understand that their share in history is shrinking. But we Americans know that our policies are in disorder, that somehow, although we can only darkly perceive this, our society is blighted. To persist in the old apocalyptic struggle would be to invite a terrifying retribution — a sterility, a poverty of response that are the sure marks of an atrophied and dying culture." — *The New Politics.*

The old contenders, in half-hearted battle, are also half in alliance with one another to defy the forces of change and renewal. Together they present a bleakly reactionary spectacle. Having once announced themselves as destiny's elect, rivals to create a new world order, they now collaborate to perpetuate the old one. They have lost their scruples, together with the pretense to universalism. The Russians long ago demonstrated their capacity for savagery, first during Stalin's regime of revolutionary necessity (as the apologists would have it), and now again in Czechoslovakia, where the cause was no universal one but old and obscurantist Russia's national need. We Americans have made our own demonstration in Indochina, devoting our most advanced technology to the manufacture of death, and to the materialization of illusion.

CHAPTER V

The Failure
of the Left

. . . revolution
Alone can save the earth from hell's pollution.

— Byron, *Don Juan*

A new age of magic interpretation of the world is coming, of interpretation in terms of the will and not of the intelligence. There is no such thing as truth, either in the moral or in the scientific sense.

— Adolf Hitler

I

T HE QUESTION IS, What is to be done? The answer begins with ideas and ideology. The political left has been the dominating and dynamic intellectual force of Western political society for two hundred years. Today that left has arrived at an intellectual impasse, and accordingly the West finds itself at a political impasse. What the left set out to do in the eighteenth century, has been accomplished. Yet people are not entirely pleased with the result. Indeed, elements of the left itself are in rebellion exactly against what has been accomplished. The left does not know what to do next. It can provide no orienting great goal, no coherent vision of further reform in Western liberal society. The political left finds itself without a program of innovation and radical reform, in a position of uneasy conservatism: it finds itself defending the status quo, because, *tant pis*, the status quo is its own best creation. This is one reason, and a central reason, why politics today, in the Western liberal states, is in such disorder, and why we are in such difficulty as we attempt to formulate a resolution of the liberal crisis.

Today's "system" in America, Canada, Britain, France, West Germany, the Low Countries, to say nothing of Scandinavia, amounts to the fulfillment *in principle and for practical purposes* of what the left has sought in the West for more than a century, and the left finds itself without a coherent program, or conception, of further structural change in our society. Thus it becomes necessary to consider whether the left, as it has existed as an intellectual and political force in recent history, may not have run its course; and whether the need today may not be for programs and innovations which in important respects contradict what the left has created and come to represent in contemporary society.

What today is described as "the system" in Western Europe and North America is the outcome of a two-hundred-year intellectual and political evolution dominated by the parties and forces of the democratic left. By the left I mean that political movement which has, since the eighteenth century, made its aims to extend political power to the masses of people and to bring about an egalitarian redistribution of wealth. Much else has attached itself to so huge and vivid an historical movement, but it is reasonable to say that these have been the two essential marks, the defining purposes, of the left.

Out of the Enlightenment, which established the secular, rationalist and scientific Western intelligence, came a political effort to unseat those political hierarchies whose justification lay in divine right. If God had not nominated Europe's monarchs, then those kings usurped power which rightly belonged — as the late eighteenth century concluded — to the people. And if political hierarchy was not divinely decreed, then neither was a related social hierarchy which made a wholly "unreasonable" allocation of wealth and privilege to the few while the masses were consigned to poverty. The Encyclopedists themselves may often have made allies of monarchs, seeking "scientific" reforms from above, uneasy about the possibilities which existed in popular upheaval, but their successors drew the necessary conclusions; and out of the Enlightenment emerged the modern left.

Radicalism had existed before — peasant rebellions, popular movements of the poor against the iniquities of power and the degradations of poverty, popular convulsions that sought a millennial release from the popular fate — but after the Enlightenment, popular unrest was placed in an entirely new moral and intellectual framework. Power and an equal share in the goods of the earth belonged to the people by right. Out of this belief, in the nineteenth century, came the modern movement of egalitarian social and political reform which appealed to the masses for support and found in the masses legitimacy, promising them liberty and an end to economic exploitation.

The left has constantly been at war with itself over how its goals should be accomplished and over the nature of the ideal society: anarchy or pure communism, both of which assume a spontaneous and effective co-operation among liberated people, or a socialist system in which the people would exercise sovereignty through a vanguard party or through elected representatives. In its debates the left steadily attracted to itself utopians, terrorists, sentimentalists and the ignorant. As George Lichtheim has remarked, ". . . until Marx came along the socialist movement was very largely run by self-educated cranks, of the kind who go about in every age endlessly repeating a few stock phrases. Marx took hold of the movement, made something out of it, and incidentally got rid of the cranks. . . . Things had been easier in the good old days when a slogan like 'Property is Theft' did duty as a political platform. After Marx one had to do some thinking."

While the drive toward economic egalitarianism was assuming the form of modern socialism, the libertarian movement was following its own political channels. Just as the feudal barons had once compelled the English monarchy to concede protoconstitutional procedures and rights to them, and townsmen had forced acknowledgment of a privileged status from the monarchy, the bourgeoisie and merchant classes of the eighteenth century adapted the New Thought to secure a political status appropriate to their economic status. They laid the groundwork for the liberal revolutions of the nineteenth century. Political power passed into the hands of the middle classes, the propertied classes, still apprehensive of democracy but now, thanks to the Enlightenment, committed to a political principle which would inevitably, by the twentieth century, culminate in the universal franchise and mass democracy.

These dual movements toward economic egalitarianism and political liberalism, each contained within them the essential principle of the other; and by our own century they had in Western Europe and the United States merged into the modern parties of the left: the Labour party, the Social Democrats, the Left-Wing Christian Democrats, and the New Deal Democratic party in the United States. More important, they had in principle won an all-party victory. Those major modern political parties with an intellectual or social ancestry on the right (or which preserve a conservative bias or class interest), all came, nonetheless, to concede the essential objectives of the parties of the left. The Tories in Britain, the postwar CDU-CSU in Germany, the American Republican party, all are committed to popular affluence, the welfare or semisocialist mixed economy (acknowledging state responsibility for assuring that the economy functions in the popular interest) and popular, democratic power, a franchise without class, sex or property qualification.

There obviously has been an illiberal left as well, but I am concerned with the mainstream Western left, which, however reluctantly at times, has committed itself to a parliamentary system created by the liberal bourgeoisie and to a competitive politics which nonetheless guarantees minority interests and individual rights. That part of the left which refused such a commitment has also failed in the West; and even in the particular conditions where it has succeeded, in the Soviet Union and Eastern Europe (areas historically cut off from the liberal West, touched only lightly if at all by the Reformation and Enlightenment), it now finds itself under certain internal political and intellectual pressures to adapt to the liberal political process.

In this century the democratic left, commanding governments, has presided over the emergence of the modern mixed economic and social systems, the system of planning and welfare, of democratic class mobility and egalitarian education — and, it must be added, of continued ruthless competition of interests, of constrained but unbroken profit-motivation in industry, of national wealth and power pursued at considerable cost to those individuals and groups unable or unwilling to compete. From one point of view this liberal left may be said to have capitulated to bourgeois and capitalist values. From another, it can be said to have won the struggle decisively, with bourgeois society itself conceding the central values and objectives of the left. There has not been a government in the industrialized West since 1945 which could be described as rightist or conservative in the meaning those terms bore in the past, or as rightist government still exists in the preliberal states of Spain, Portugal and Greece. Konrad Adenauer and Charles de Gaulle, or even Dwight Eisenhower, might properly be described as conservative in temperament and style, but their political programs were egalitarian and democratic. Their conservativism was a matter of conserving (if not to extend) the system of one man-one vote, mass affluence, classlessness, the limiting or removal of gross and institutionalized discrepancies in private wealth.

Many commentators on the left will bitterly resist this argument, insisting that the left has only partially and fragmentarily affected Western politics and government. They point not only to the poverty, the sectors of human blight, which survive in the midst of the riches of Western Europe and North America, but also to the effective political disenfranchisement of sizable groups within these states. They emphasize the continued power of capitalism, the influence of inherited wealth, the persistence — indeed the institutionalizing — of privilege. They correctly argue that American congressmen and European parliamentary deputies represent the privilege and special interests within their districts, sectors of wealth and the source of campaign monies, as often as they do any seriously conceived popular interest. They condemn the rotten boroughs which still exist, and the seniority system in the American Congress, which has given inordinate power to the representatives of rural, one-party, racially biased districts. They note the profound institutional conservatism, not to say reaction, of governmental bureaucracies.

They say that the American workingman pays proportionately higher taxes than the rich and receives proportionately less — in social services, medical care, police protection, security. They note that the programs of the welfare state inveterately tend to become subsidies for privilege: for industrial rather than family farms; speculative builders rather than individuals in need of housing; highway builders and transportation corporations rather than the workingmen who need public transport; the securely unionized worker rather than the common laborer, the migrant worker, the individual craftsman; the middle-class student rather than the culturally crippled slum child; the food-processing company while in the United States actual starvation and disabling malnutrition exist among thousands. They call attention to the fact that there has been no significant change in the distribution of wealth in the United States since World War II, and that even when the poor or disenfranchised in Western society mobilize to protest their condition, they often enough meet a frankly repressive counteraction.

Yet the only possible reply is that this surely is evidence not of the continued domination of the right, but of the compromises made by the left in the course of political success, evidence of inadequacies or shortfalls in the very national policies conceived by the left. All of this is an aspect of the competitive Lockean political mechanism — that political marketplace in which individual liberty has been purchased at a not inconsiderable cost. Obviously such a "success" by the left as I have described leaves much — "everything" — to be completed in practice. But it also amounts to as much of a success as any political movement ever enjoys. The left has established the goals of modern society, it dominates the form and assumptions of modern government — most of all, it dominates the political imagination and intelligence of the age.

I I

Yet the established parties of the left, with their principles almost universally conceded, their fundamental programs widely accomplished, today discover that the public is restless and resentful. The public is critical of their achievements and of the system they have created. The young savagely attack them as part of the hated "system," and defect to romanticism and violence. The old Democratic party and socialist voters prove unexpectedly vulnerable to the appeal of the conservative opposition — to consolidate the welfare society, to economize and retrench. These voters even prove susceptible to a New Populism directed exactly against the distant liberal and socialist "establishment."

There are endless explanations of why this reaction should take place, but the fundamental reason seems to me this: the most important new political and social issues being felt within the industrial societies today fall outside the traditional categories of the left. They are no longer, primarily, economic issues, and the tradition of the left has been to define politics in economic and class categories. They reflect, as we have seen, anxieties of identity and social community. They are marked by an ambivalence about technology — the source of egalitarian affluence — and a reaction (often blind, but increasingly influential) against the centralization of authority in modern society, the anonymity of power, and — perhaps most of all — the apparent escape of power from reasonable control.

For a great many people there is a sense of individual powerlessness in the midst of seemingly limitless material and organizational power. Nothing seems to work properly. Confidence in the rational administration of society is seriously weakened even among the liberal and professional intelligentsia, which, traditionally, have made this the indispensable core of their political beliefs.*

To put it practically, and in terms of the American debate, good intentions have produced Vietnam, and Vietnam is American liberalism's war. The Republican Administrations of the 1950's specifically refused to intervene with military power in Vietnam, even though President Eisenhower was placed under heavy pressures to do so. It took a visionary liberal Administration fully to translate the globalism of American rhetoric, which the Republican party wholly shared, into a program of national action. Vietnam was consciously made into a test of liberal international reform by the Kennedy and Johnson Administrations — of liberal "nation building,"

---

* We can afford amusement at Lenin's conviction — before taking power in Russia — that the administration of a nation and of its economy could largely be reduced "to very simple operations such as registration, filing, and checking. Hence they will be quite within the reach of every literate person." But the sophisticated and pragmatic Fabians are rather closer to us. The Webbs, Beatrice and Sidney (who spent their honeymoon investigating Dublin trade societies; —

> What fun that happy couple had
> As with a gentle laugh
> They added and subtracted
> Then drew another graph)

and Bernard Shaw, Graham Wallas, Sydney Olivier, based their immensely influential movement — incubator of Britain's modern Labour governments — upon the supremely self-evident proposition that only good will, straight thinking and political persistence were necessary to remake industrial Britain. "'Socialism is nothing else but common sense," said Olivier.

carried on behind a shield of Green Beret counterinsurgent warfare — against the Asian Communist "model" of radical national transformation.

Technology produces thermonuclear bombs, ballistic and antiballistic missiles. Industry makes cheap goods, but wrecks the landscape and pollutes the air and rivers. Technocrats insist that all problems are soluble, but their schemes persistently misfire; they manufacture bacteriological and nerve gases, have accidents with them, lie about the accidents, don't know how safely to dispose of the poisons once they have made them. Experts' programs of urban reconstruction and racial reform enlarge the slums, radicalize the poor, and jeopardize the security of a middle stratum of white workers and civil servants who have themselves just escaped the ghettos. Bureaucracies meddle in private lives, humiliating the poor. Medical progress underwrites a population growth which crushes our communities, yet medical care is all but absent from the poorest communities and exorbitantly expensive for the middle classes. Mass education produces a million yahoos, undermining high culture, and at the same time cannot teach reading and arithmetic to the slum child. The centers of urban civilization itself, cities and the liberal universities, begin to disintegrate under these pressures. The middle classes complain that the police cannot protect them, that the garbage cannot reliably be collected or the trains kept running. The poor complain that the police are their enemies, that the police condone the drug trade and ignore the petty criminals who prey on them, and that the authorities hardly try to clean their streets or enforce the health and building codes for their benefit; and even among the unpoliticized poor there appears to be a distinct rise in nihilistic social behavior.

These complaints are made worse by the fact that they often arise out of the very effort to resolve them. Public grievances are provoked by reform programs which fail, or by partial reform successes which intensify the grievances of those still unaided. Poverty, for example, is a practical, definable issue, by definition susceptible of economic solution in the great tradition of the left. Yet the persistence of poverty in American society, as Nathan Glazer has argued, no longer is really a political matter in the sense of involving a deliberate choice among coherent alternative courses of action. There are few Americans, and no major American political movement, arguing the necessity or inevitability of a poor proletariat in America. Few Americans, for that matter, will explicitly defend racial inequities, to say nothing of racial discrimination, as a matter of principle or social necessity (or inevitability). But there is a profound difficulty amounting almost to despair over *how* to make a great change in either situation. The problem is how to do what nearly everyone agrees should be done. Underlying the surface debates — guaranteed income versus black capitalism, bureaucratic reform versus community control, politicization of the poor communities versus programs of family support and social welfare — is deep uncertainty over what any of these programs can really accomplish. Whether it is justified or not, and in considerable measure it may be unjustified,* there is among the public a persistent sense of the futility of these measures.

There *ought* to be a way to get income to the urban poor. People believe there *ought* to be a way to get schools

---

* As in the case of black living standards, income and education in the United States, which over the past decade have in fact shown a steady improvement, disproportionately more rapid than the increase for whites.

that work for the poor, and decent housing. It ought, above all, to be possible to build houses and reconstruct the basic social services of the city — housing, medical service, street cleaning and garbage collection, cheap mass transportation. Whatever the present rhetoric or historical reality of institutionalized racism in this country, there has since the 1950's been an unmistakable American national commitment to racial change. No doubt the popular commitment is gradualist, antiradical, integrative rather than separatist; no doubt there is plenty of residual racial hostility, as well as panicky official repressions of black radicalism. But in this matter the reality today is a community of frustration, of shared impotence.

Overwrought or overstated though the public sense of impotence often may be, there is too much truth in it for comfort. It is not simply the complaint of a minority or of the intelligentsia, but increasingly it is expressed by very large numbers of people. There is, additionally, moral anxiety — a pervasive sense, born of these injustices and cases of incompetence, and of the bewildering simultaneous commitment of modern governments to social welfare and to hyperbolic, and intrinsically irrational, modes of war, that society has lost its moral direction and for that reason its moral authority.

Where is moral assurance or security to be found? When American "Minutemen" cache rifles and train themselves to the guerrilla defense of their families, and black students removed from the urban slums to American universities arm themselves, they are in some degree reacting to this loss of moral security. They are preparing to defend themselves against (nameless?) menaces which political authority can no longer be relied upon to prevent. If there is no security within the political system, men must act for themselves. This is a profound sign of the breakdown of the political order.

I I I

The established parties of the Western left regard this contradictory spectacle with uneasiness. It is their doing, the seemingly blighted outcome of their struggle and success. They do not know what to do next. They can feel no confidence about the future. Their traditional programs have been put into practice: centralized economic and social planning, the institution of the managed economy and welfare social policy, centralization of political authority and the application of technocratic expertise to directing the nation — these are realities in all the Western liberal states. They are the accomplishments of the New Deal and Fair Deal in America, of Great Britain's Fabian theorists and the Labour government of 1945, of the Socialist-Center-party coalitions of postwar Western Europe.

Yet in the midst of their "success," the left experiences rebellion on its own left, a serious defection of its traditional voters to parties on the right, and disorientation, conflict, among its leaders over fundamental issues of program and direction. The Democrats in the United States, Labour in Britain, the Socialists on the Continent — none seem able today to agree on programs which promise more than a dull recapitulation and marginal, if indispensable, extension of their own old policies. In 1968 in America it was Mr. Humphrey who seemed the reactionary figure, the sunny New Deal optimist evading his inheritance of war and American moral crisis. The European Socialists, when they are not in coalition with the Center

or Conservative parties, have only token programs of
further socialism, further nationalization; they understand that the further nationalization of industry will
change little of any consequence. The Brandt government
in Germany justifies itself by foreign policy innovation,
not domestic reform of any scale or novelty. The younger
theorists of the mainstream parties of the left produce
sensible but lifeless programs of incidental reform, re-
furbishings of the New Deal or Labour party or social-
democratic programs of the 1930's. Even the most visionary theorists from within the established left, calling for
a new democratic socialism able to "abolish compulsory
work and the rationing system of money" (to cite the goals
of the American socialist Michael Harrington), fail to
awaken the slightest response from the masses. Even their
fellow socialists seem hardly convinced. It is not simply
that we all have been co-opted to the system by affluence
(that alibi of radicalism). Money issues — doing away
with money, making it available without "compulsory
work" — simply no longer go to the heart of things. Such
promises no longer dazzle us; they may even make us a little anxious.

Moreover, all of the new programs from within the old
left rely for their fulfillment on some revival of the old alliance between workers and the liberal middle classes,
a new "conscience constituency" to be held together by
idealism rather than class and economic struggle. The
old left — of the nineteenth century, of the New Deal
and modern trade unionism — was built on the humilia-
tions and human need of an oppressed working class. Its
leadership more often than not was provided by idealistic, conscience-stricken, middle-class intellectuals, and
it could depend on a crucial increment of political and

The Failure of the Left

moral support from within the bourgeoisie and the established intelligentsia. Today the decline in urgency of the economic issue, the very achievement of the old left in breaking down class barriers and moving workers into a classless middle class, has dealt a critical blow to that alliance. As the 1968 election in America and the British election of 1970 have demonstrated, the mass of wage earners cannot reasonably be expected to be more liberal on racial issues, or more tolerant of painful social reforms, less chauvinist or conventional in their foreign policy views, than the society as a whole. Increasingly the tangible interests, the real grievances, of workingmen — these "forgotten men" of the new liberal society — have pushed them in quite other directions.

Unionizing the unorganized poor could still affect the political complexion of the established trade-union and socialist movement, reviving — for a time at least — the old alliance of social reformers with workingmen in real need. The fact, though, is that the established unions are hardly interested in the unorganized poor — unreliable and troublesome recruits, threats to labor's own "system." The unions in general have become profoundly conservative organizations. They restrict apprenticeship, protect their own privileges (look after the lads), co-operate with industry within a formalized ritual combat which takes place each time the contract is renegotiated; and they regard with frank hostility those who would rock this arrangement.

The unions have become pillars of the Establishment, and it is not surprising that this is so. It is the illusion of theorists and ideologues that the mass of workingmen, organized or unorganized, should be notably less selfish than the bourgeoisie. Why should they? Once the workingman has won a position of basic economic security, and reasonable expectations, he has considerably more reason to be conservative on social issues than the middle-class executive or professional man with investments or an unearned income. For the workingman, *everything* could be jeopardized by radical change. Thus George Meany — and Harold Wilson — and even such old-line European Communist chieftians as Jacques Duclos, nostalgic about past struggles but the resolute enemies of New Left, student radicals, Maoists and Marxist revisionists, are perfectly appropriate leaders of their movements, faithful to their working-class followers.

If the West again experiences economic crisis, a new depression, unemployment, we will again have a radical labor movement, and the old alliance with liberal theorists and social reformers will spring to life again. It will as quickly then fall back into conservatism as the economic demands of the workers are met, when the worker is provided with the security which allows him again to become what he wants most to be, an ordinary bloody-minded man living a life of private gratifications, family satisfactions, a comfortably conventional view of the world.

In a tacit concession of this point, some theorists of a new socialism, or in America of a "New Politics," have recast their notion of the liberal voting alliance so as to allot the primary role to a new "intellectual proletariat" of college-educated clerks, bureaucratic and corporate technicians and managers, suburban executives, whose education and status supposedly make them socially progressive (the New Left would argue to the contrary that they are the occasionally restless but ultimately obedient agents of the Establishment). These are the people who make up the Reform Democrats in America, the new Tories in Britain. Willy Brandt has recruited them to his SDP in Germany; Jean-Jacques Servan-Schreiber has tried to make them the core of a new French coalition of reform (by assiduously imitating the Kennedy style, already out of fashion in its native country). They have responded in the past to the appeals of Pierre Mendès-France, to Eugene McCarthy and Adlai Stevenson. In America today they provide the articulate cadres of the nonparty reform and antiwar movements.

Yet what is most striking about this "conscience constituency" is that its members do not respond to the leadership of the old left or the familiar programs of welfare state or socialism. Theirs is an ambivalent political class, perhaps an ideologically inchoate one. They are skeptical of the unions, hostile to the old parties. They are (in America) "neo-isolationist" in their foreign policy views. They are disillusioned with the old political style of sweeping reforms and centralized power. Undeniably they constitute a "coalition for change" — but for change in what direction? The style and temper, the overall political thrust, of the McCarthy movement in America in 1968 — so influential in the suburbs and among the professional intelligentsia — was actually conservative. Senator McCarthy wanted to reduce presidential power, not increase it. He wanted to provide cabinet officers with unprecedented authority, to devolve federal power downward and outward from the Washington center. He wanted to "liberate individuals so that they may determine their own lives." He said, "This is a good country if the President will just let it be." The really new elements in the "New Politics" seem ultimately conservative. They include ideas of social reform whose effect would change the present system more radically than anything seriously proposed from the parties of the old left, yet the movement itself reveals a sharp break with the established traditions of the left.

I V

Out of this dilemma of the left, the New Left reaction has emerged, instinctively taking as its chief enemy not the right but the old left — the "liberal establishment."

In considering the New Left it is necessary first to distinguish black militancy from the (predominately white) New Left — the international, and avowedly revolutionary, movement of students and a radical Western intelligentsia. The militancy which has arisen within America's black population is easy to comprehend, although on the American historical record it may prove the hardest matter to resolve. It is easy to understand because it amounts to a familiar case of struggle by an oppressed class for an equal role in society. It is quite within the classical pattern of the Western past, a drive for economic and political equality. This is essentially true even when the struggle assumes, as it now tends to do, the form of a "nationalist" movement seeking black autonomy and vindication of the black identity and personality. It requires no feat of the white imagination to understand what blacks want, or what the full social and economic integration of the black community in America would imply. (Or, for that matter, what black separatism would be like, if that were realizable.) Nor are practical remedies for black grievances hard to find, although their application is crucially difficult. As a popular movement the black struggle, like that of the Spanish-speaking and Indian minorities, is perfectly reasonable: the fundamental goals are identifiable, tangible, achievable. We are not required to transform our consciousness, or acquire a revolutionary sensibility, in order to solve these problems. We merely have to provide jobs, housing, education, equal treatment and status in the economy and under the law, for America's racial minorities. The militancy of a part of the black leadership may assume illiberal forms, but the character of the movement as a whole is quite within the political bounds and experience of liberal society: it does not represent a qualitatively new phenomenon in our political culture.

At the same time the consequences of failure in dealing with this matter are also clear, since denial of the realizable and just demands of a mobilized tenth of the American population must imply either an unprecedented and deliberate program of repression by the majority, the violent collapse of the national society, or the human catastrophe of a moral disintegration within the American black community. It is difficult to say which is the more probable, except that it is not likely to be national collapse — a society will not bear anarchy for long, whatever the terrors and costs of the alternatives.

With the revival of a revolutionary left in the West, and a radicalization among the young and the intelligentsia, we have genuinely new factors in the contempory situation. How new? The Western nations have before gone through times of controversy over social injustices, the merits of a colonial war, over the values and competence of a ruling establishment, without any revolutionary outcome. The search for appropriate historical analogies by both the adherents of the new movement and the new sensibility and their critics is significant in itself. For the Oxford historian Max Beloff, the students resemble the pre-Fascist and Fascist young of Europe in the 1920's. For the American sociologist Lewis Feuer, they belong to that tradition of young "historicists, terrorists, totalitarians, and anti-Semites" who wrecked the cause of German freedom in the nineteenth century and again in the 1920's, who fatally disrupted Czarist Russia's evolution toward constitutionalism, who recurrently act out in politics an Oedipal slaying of their fathers. For Theodore Roszak, a sympathetic critic of the movement, what is being created by the young is a new culture — a "counterculture" — comparable to the Renaissance in its potentialities. For Paul Goodman, the young recall Luther reacting against the corruption and intellectual irrelevance of Rome in 1510; they are the new Protestants. For some American critics — notably the President and the Vice President — what the country is experiencing is simply subversion, the well-intentioned young being exploited to block an antitotalitarian American foreign policy. For some of the extravagantly committed in the New Left it is 1938 again, the storm troopers gathering to attack, and "we are all Jews."

The analogies, mostly unconvincing, are both political and cultural, yet there is no doubt that what we are dealing with here is in its widest version the product of cultural estrangement. Such radical writers as the English psychiatrist R. D. Laing, Roszak and even Herbert Marcuse really represent no true political movement, but an attack against certain crucial values of modern society and the modern intellect. They advocate overthrow of the rule of the technocrat and expert, which is to say, the rule of rationalism. The movement they represent, Roszak says, "has turned from objective consciousness as if from a place inhabited by plague . . . one can just begin to see an entire episode of our cultural history, the great age of science and technology which began with the Enlightenment, standing revealed in all its quaintly arbitrary, often absurd, and all too painfully unbalanced aspects." But is such an assertion worth attention? Roszak commends to us a "shamanistic" world view, giving direct voice to the quasi-religious or neo-religious longings and ambitions which are an important element in the "countercultural" movement.* Laing suggests that rationalist society may be mad, and the mad the only sane ones among us: Dr. Caligari rules the asylum. What has this to do with politics? The final allusion suggests that it has a great deal to do with it.

The radical intellectual critique begins with the barrenness of popular culture and the anomic or alienated conditions of individual life in industrial societies. It reacts against tangible social injustices. It analyzes the established system's responsibility for those conditions. A good many of its charges are undeniable. The university abuses which touched off the student rebellion in the 1960's were, for the most part, inexcusable: class discrim-

---

* The argument that the "counter-cultural" element in the New Left — and the essential thrust of the related drug culture — is religious in character, made by many of the movement's supporters and observers, is curiously insensitive to the historical character of Western religion. The orthodox traditions, both Jewish and Christian, have held that religion is not a matter of "sensible consolations" or mystical good feelings but of willing submission to hard demands, to what often seems the arbitrary will of God. Western religion traditionally involves the practice of virtue, achieved through sacrifice, suffering — and in the Christian tradition, of humility, mortification, the abandonment of private will: difficult things, not easy ones. Thus Christian mysticism did not promise "cosmic consciousness" or "mind expansion," but aridity, spiritual testing, John of the Cross's "dark night of the soul." The "religious" tendency of the New Left's counter-culture is, rather, suggestive of Pelagianism, the heresy of the natural perfectibility of man and the denial of original sin. Instead of making a challenge to the historical and moral optimism of the liberal tradition, the New Left reaffirms it at a new and intensified level of quasi-religious belief.

ination, bad facilities and overcrowding in the Italian and French education systems, bureaucratic and professorial abuses there and in the United States. The student demand that the universities be devoted to learning rather than to train — as auxiliaries of the national economy — technicians and bureaucrats (training for "brain sales"; the function of the "multiversity") could as well be argued by traditional scholars (as it is, for example, by F. R. Leavis, no New Left militant). The German students' criticism of press monopolies was justified, and their argument in 1968 that creation of the Grand Coalition had foreclosed practical political opposition within the parliamentary system had the support of a good many other observers of German politics. In short, none of these were inherently radical issues, to say nothing of "revolutionary" ones — although the student style might romantically have been adapted from Cuban or Spartacist models.

Even many of the avowedly "revolutionary" demands remain within a recognizable tradition of Western liberal politics, as when the German student leader Rudi Dutschke explains what he seeks: "Every citizen must be answerable to himself. He must be convinced that his vote is necessary and good — not useless, the way it is today. The revolution will end the manipulation of masses by those with power. . . . First we must produce changed men. The future has no place for an elite establishment. People do not want to be led, but to be answerable for their own actions."

But how to change men? Or even to describe what their revolutionary institutions really might be? Here, of course, the New Left has consistently faltered, driven to recall the Paris Commune or to exalt a sentimental anarchism (sentimental because, as the distinguished anarchist writer Paul Goodman has insisted, the movement typically refuses to accept the responsibilities of anarchism: to deal seriously with the problems of work and production, of professionalism, of self-government on a modern scale), or a fancifully imagined version of Maoism or Castroism.*

While the American radical movement has been dominated by the overriding issue of the Vietnam war — and the extent to which that war is an "inevitable" product of modern American racism, capitalism and neo-imperialism — the European movement formulated a much wider critique. The motivating issues are bound up in technological society itself. There is the creation by modern industrialism of a new "underclass" (a nonproletariat?) of technological unemployables, discards of society (while technology's jobs are for the educated and intellectually adept, thus co-opting them to the system). There is the mobilization of the universities — of learning and science — to purposes of state and industrial development, dominated by an elite which refuses (or is structurally unable) to make itself accountable to the masses. This elite makes use of the mass media to further a "tol-

---

* Goodman writes of a dialogue with New York graduate students in 1967: "[I found] they did not believe in the existence of real professions at all; professions were concepts of repressive society and 'linear thinking.' I asked them to envisage any social order they pleased — Mao's, Castro's, some anarchist utopia — and wouldn't there be engineers who knew about materials and stresses and strains? Wouldn't people get sick and need to be treated? Wouldn't there be problems of communication? No, they insisted; it was important only to be human, and all else would follow.

"Suddenly I realized that they did not really believe that there was a nature of things. Somehow all functions could be reduced to interpersonal relations and power. There was no knowledge, but only the sociology of knowledge . . . they did not believe there was such a thing as simple truth. To be required to learn something was a trap by which the young were put down and co-opted. Then I knew that I could not get through to them."

erant repression," even a "systemic Fascism" which has
no need for the old Fascist brutalities because the socio-
political structure itself forecloses the possibilities of
radical resistance, and the masses are "narcotized" by
consumer affluence. How has all this come about? By
the conditions of industrial power and production — frag-
mentary work, urbanization, alienation from creative
work — by the surplus production of socially useless
goods showered upon masses who are induced by advertising to believe in a vast series of artificial "needs."
It comes about by the centralization of power imposed
by industrial (and political) rationalization, and through
the resources for social control and manipulation which
technology has made available to government and the
economy's managers. What, then, is to be done? Break
or tame the technology — break the system. The first steps
are to defy its standards, to awaken an anti-industrial
consciousness, to confront the system's contradictions
and unmask its latent ferocity, making its nature plain to
the masses.

A common theme in much of the radical movement is
the quest for a restored "wholeness" to life, for a revival
of intuition and impulse, of spontaneity in personal relations and fulfillment, creativity, in work. There is in this
a notable resemblance to past conservative and romantic
critiques of industrialism, made as late as in the 1930's
and 1940's, among Southern writers in the United States
and by conservative and Catholic intellectuals in Europe,
nostalgic for the preindustrial values of past "integral"
societies. At Vanderbilt University among the Southern
"agrarian" poets and critics (whose political manifesto,
famous in its day, was called *I'll Take My Stand*), in neo-

Thomist circles in France, in the cultural criticisms of men such as T. S. Eliot and Wyndham Lewis and Georges Bernanos, and earlier among the Georgian poets and pre-Raphaelites of England, and the German youth movements, the *Wandervögel* and the followers of Stefan George, much the same judgments were made upon industrial society's impact on individual lives and upon a humane social order. Much the same vision of true values was proclaimed, except that those critics argued that a society of "wholeness" had once existed (or a closer approach to it) in eighteenth-century England or thirteenth-century France or pre-Wilhelmine Germany, or in the agrarian ante-bellum American South. The new radicals, their eyes on the future, are not at all clear in describing the practical implications of their vision (a society possessing a shamanistic world view irresistibly brings to mind D. H. Lawrence — his neo-primitivist Mexico of *The Plumed Serpent* with an admixture of hallucinogenic mushrooms and rock music), or they are politically disquieting when, as in the writings of Marcuse, they try to spell it out. Yet many of them ought not, one would think, be unhappy with G. K. Chesterton's and Hilaire Belloc's mythical England of beef, beer and good poetry — except that an unmistakable note of Puritanism persists in what the new cultural critics write, notwithstanding their avowals of sexual liberation and their discarding of "surplus" repression.

V

The fact that this line of criticism of modern society has such antecedents raises the question of whether we see here simply an intelligentsia's established distaste for industrial mass society.* Or is it really something new, after all, and are the young people who articulate these criticisms and go on to mobilize a political attack on modern society really a vanguard? Are they really the articulators of discontents which in less focused versions have been deeply and extensively felt within industrial society for a century past? On the face of it, one would say no. The French students of 1968, who tried, failed to create anything more than an ephemeral alliance with the French workers, and they outraged the bourgeoisie. The American New Left has no working-class sympathizers except for some black militants (and this, one suspects, is a transient alliance rather than any true joining of interests); the American laboring man seems, if anything, in the vanguard of the antileft movement.

The New Left has never cohered as a serious, popular, political movement because it has never been able to master the problem of defining a program which could appeal beyond the intelligentsia to a politically important sector of the Western populations. Unlike the old socialists, the Communist party, the old anarchists,† the New Left makes no convincing appeal to people outside the intellectual and generational ghettos from which it first emerged.

---

* As Maurice Cranston has savagely described Herbert Marcuse: he recoils "from the *Untermenschen*. . . . The idea of mankind appeals to him; real men — most of them — sicken him. For this reason it is as difficult to believe in his anarchism as it is, for other reasons, to believe in his Marxism. . . . Marcuse has the stomach of a very high-class aesthete, queasy, fastidious, and misanthropic."

† Anarchism could still be a popular workingman's movement as late as turn-of-the-century America — in the Industrial Workers of the World, the "Wobblies" — and as late as the 1930's in Spain, where thousands of ordinary men died, or were sacrificed by their fellows on the left, in the anarchist battalions of the Spanish Civil War.

Even its utopianism is of a kind which limits its appeal: the specifically political arguments of a Marcuse or of a Noam Chomsky affront the common sense of the workingman — as the arguments of Big Bill Haywood, Tom Watson, or of Trotsky and Lenin, did not. These men could say what they wanted of the world, and make an intelligible argument about how to get it. The New Left describes an intellectualized elysium — when it is able to describe its social goals at all in terms other than revolutionary rhetoric, or by reference to hopelessly romanticized pictures of Cuban or Chinese reality, preposterous to an American or European workingman. The intellectual absolutism of the New Left thrusts them away from the ordinary people who may share many of the anxieties which underlie the movement.

The New Left often reflects a disillusioned technocratic temperament, as in the case of Chomsky, a radical optimist who might be said to have unexpectedly discovered sin but not original sin. Like many in the New Left, his belatedly awakened horror at the Vietnam war compelled him to elaborate a universal theory of linked imperialism and liberal elites, assiduously suppressing popular revolutions whether they appeared in Germany of the 1920's, Spain of the 1930's, Cuba of the 1950's or Asia in the 1960's. But popular revolution remains in his writings, as in the writings of Gabriel Kolko and Susan Sontag, a suspiciously sentimental category, embracing American black nationalists, Asian peasants and Spanish anarchists; libertarians and terrorists; campus activists and Rosa Luxemburg. Herbert Marcuse, of course, contemptuously writes off the "narcotized" urban masses and places his trust in students and the intelligentsia. He is another utopian optimist in an age whose clearest lesson, commonly appreciated by the ordinary people who have been its victims, has been dystopian.

In this respect the argument made by the American radical historian Christopher Lasch is worth attention, that there will never be a relevant American socialism — if there is to be one — unless it is derived from the indigenous American tradition of radical populism, expressing "the needs of people whose lives . . . [are] controlled by institutions over which they . . . [have] a steadily diminishing amount of power." Lasch, significantly, has only contempt for the "mindless revolutionary militancy based on irrelevant models" of the present-day American New Left.

V I

Yet where is the genuinely valid model — for Americans or Europeans? The doctrinal problem of the New Left can be simply put, and it derives from the dilemma of the established left we have already examined. The truth is that, historically, the left in its old quest for popular prosperity and popular democracy has found only two realizable solutions. The one is social democracy, "liberal welfarism," with all of its compromises to privilege and the acquisitive instinct, along with its centralized bureaucracies of power and its planning boards and technocrats, and the other is Leninism with its fatal sacrifice of liberty. Is there a Third Way? The East European and Italian Marxist revisionists have made the most serious effort to find the Third Way — the least sentimental, the most responsible effort — yet their way keeps coming out as some modification of social democracy.

The Failure of the Left

Of the two historical solutions, both are abhorrent to the New Left. They don't want Leninism. And social democracy, whatever its potentialities for reform, still is exactly the hated "system" against which they are in rebellion. It is noteworthy that the French New Left, in its moment of revolutionary triumph in Paris in 1968, seemed virtually to re-enact the ideological history of the left, frantically sifting through all of the old and discarded experiments of Proudhon and Kropotkin, of doctrinaire Populism and anarchism, to end up either in intellectual abdication — the revolution will make itself — or confronting the hated alternatives of liberal social democracy and Leninism.

But the New Left already has slipped into factionalism, despite the anti-ideological convictions of that wing of the movement responsible for launching the student protests. The anti-ideological wing itself is driven toward the philosophy of the immanent act, arguing that political meaning resides in *being* a revolutionary, and consequences are beyond account. This, too, is not new: consider André Breton in the *Second Surrealist Manifesto*, of 1930: "The simple surrealist act would consist of going out into the street, revolver in hand, and firing at random into the crowd as long as one could."

It is not hard to feel sympathy for the young Maoists and Trotskyites who have attempted to take control of the New Left. Possessing a political doctrine with serious antecedents and a realistic approach to power, they, at least, understand that programs and organization are essential in a political offensive, to say nothing of a revolution. They grasp that the New Left as a whole, born out of a reaction against the uses of power, consistently shrinks from the implications of organizing to seize and use power. There are — there can be — no Lenins among the New Left so long as the movement keeps its present predominant character, and its present character is that it lacks not only a program for taking power but *the will to power*.*

The motives of the New Left are libertarian and egalitarian; but, frustrated, its activists increasingly are intoxicated with violence, with the possibilities of a cleansed and purged world, a new Reign of Virtue. Max Beloff describes them as Fascists, acting in "a mythological twilight where it can be asserted that, provided one's feelings are sincere and held with passion, the choices need not be made and Utopia can come about as a mere by-product . . . of . . . destruction." But despite what he charges, theirs is not a Fascist politics as we have known it — how consoling that would be to the beleaguered old liberals and socialists they attack! — though it is the Fascist sensibility: visionary, committed to purity of feeling, anti-intellectual, antipragmatic, seduced by the "aristocratic charms" (as Yves Simon once put it) of nihilism.

However, the new Left will not take over the world,

* The New Left's canonization of Che Guevara is a telling fact. Surely he represents revolutionary death, not life — failure, not success. His Bolivian campaign was an exemplary case of sheer, and even willful, incompetence, a search not for power but for martyrdom. Poor Che! — who couldn't speak the language of the Indians he wanted to save, who lost his asthma medicine, his records, his supplies, his maps, his way, his life. The whole New Left commitment to Third World revolution is sentimental, a largely unreciprocated love affair. Vietnamese, Algerian, Peruvian rebels have perfectly comprehensible and conventional goals: power, in order to remake national societies by "modernizing" them — which means building sophisticated economies, armies, centralized governments, re-creating the conditions against which the urban rebels of New York and Paris, and Prague, are reacting. The Third World rebels, whatever their illusions, deal in life and death in the real world. The young Westerners, culturally alienated rebels, would appropriate to themselves something of the supposed simplicity, solidarity and austerity of the preindustrial Third World.

or even the universities. Its hostility to serious programs is an inherent bar to success, even if the ambition of alliance with the industrial working class were not fantasy. It trades on the inhibitions of liberal government, a wrecking tactic of great importance. The power of the weak, whether it is in Vietnam or at the university, depends upon the contradiction that the powerful will not use their ultimate means of power. But there is a penultimate threshold: the powerful can violate their avowed values and repress, jail, terrorize; the powerful can make total war. The war in Vietnam, like the war in the universities and cities, could be "won" in a way that would vindicate New Left theory while eliminating the theorists.

By exploiting the political paradoxes in the power of the weak, the radicals acquire very considerable influence, and their moral effect on liberal governments and the Western public as a whole has already been given a convincing demonstration. But the movement's positive power — its power to articulate, to say nothing of calling into being, an alternative organization of modern society — is negligible. Unlike the revolutionary movements of 1789 or 1917 the new radicals have, and seemingly can have, no creative issue capable of evoking a mass response. However romantic or "unrealistic" — or ignorant — the Jacobins were, they had an issue: popular sovereignty. However intolerant or naïve the Leninists were, they proved to be supremely opportunist tacticians of power, and again, they had an issue: power to the workingmen's "soviets," which existed in the factories, workshops and the army. Insofar as the American radicals have a positive issue, it seems to be the abolition of power itself.

The abolition of power is not a political program but

121

antipolitics: an affirmation of nihilism. It is an articulation of despair. It is the intellectual outcome of blasted idealism, repudiating the moral intelligibility which makes a human society possible in the very name of morality. It contributes to a contemporary situation in which deep mechanisms of anxiety and moral insecurity have come into play among the Western publics, and in which the metapolitical response becomes possible: the advent of a leadership which promises no mere competence and order, but a new meaning to life itself, which will promise — as a Sorbonne poster of 1968 demanded — to "transform life itself."

There is a deeper congruence between the despair, revealed in a frantic optimism, which is the inner dynamic of the New Left, and the restless search for justice and for *connection,* coherence, which animates the New Populism. The New Left is giving idiosyncratic, even avantgarde, expression to the new anxieties of the modern liberal society. It was born not simply of the colonial war of a liberal nation but from widely shared anxieties arising out of the conditions of individual life in a society experiencing social dissolution and incompetent structures; it gives desperate, even poignant, expression — quoting the Port Huron statement of American students in 1962 — to "loneliness, estrangement, isolation."

CHAPTER VI

The Future of Ideology

When fighting for your truth, you must take care not to kill it with the very arms you are using to defend it — only under such double conditions do words resume their living meaning. Knowing that, the intellectual has the role of distinguishing in each camp the respective limits of force and justice. That role is to clarify definitions in order to disintoxicate minds and to calm fanaticisms, even when this is against the current tendency.

— Albert Camus

I

THE "NEW" ANXIETIES
felt among the liberal societies today arise out of conservative longings; they are not a true phenomenon of
the left. The complaint, the critique being voiced, under
its veneer of contemporary language, is hardly distinguishable from the attack which for a century and a half has
been made by the right against democracy, liberalism, the
legacies of the Enlightenment. Depersonalization, dissolution of social bonds, dissociation of individuals from
tradition and community, secularization, the idolatry of
science, the abusive centralization of power: we might as
well be recounting, refining into modern terms, the
established European conservative's critique, even the reactionary's attack upon the modern liberal world.

Tocqueville, the sympathetic observer of nineteenth-
century American democracy, nonetheless supplied this
description of what we might call "repressive tolerance":
noting the "immense and tutelary power" of the American central government, he said that it

> every day renders the exercise of the free agency of man
> less useful and less frequent; it circumscribes the will
> within a narrower range and gradually robs a man of
> all the uses of himself. The principle of equality has
> prepared men for these things; it has predisposed men
> to endure them and often to look on them as benefits.
> . . . Such a power does not destroy, but it prevents
> existence; it does not tyrannize, but it compresses,
> enervates, extinguishes, and stupefies a people, till each

125

nation is reduced to nothing better than a flock of timid and industrious animals, of which the government is the shepherd.

I have always thought that servitude of the regular, quiet, and gentle kind which I have just described might be combined more easily than is commonly believed with some of the outward forms of freedom, and that it might even establish itself under the wing of the sovereignty of the people.

Writing of Europe after the 1848 revolutions, and of the argument that revolutionary centralizations of power are followed in a "pendular motion" by power's decentralization, Tocqueville says on another occasion that "the last word always rests with centralization, which grows deeper even when it seems less apparent on the surface, since the social movement, the *atomization* and the *isolation* of social elements, always continues during such times." (The emphasis is Tocqueville's.)

Or read Jacob Burckhardt, the Swiss pessimist and nineteenth-century prophet of an age of *"terribles simplificateurs* who are going to descend upon poor old Europe":

> The chief phenomenon of our days is the sense of the provisional. In addition to the uncertainty of each individual's fate we are confronted with a colossal problem of existence whose elements must be viewed . . . as *new consequences and tendencies arisen from the revolution* [of 1789].
>
> . . . Part of this general process was a *lawless centralization* which had arisen in a time of "danger to the fatherland." This centralization has existed in complete form even in the monarchies only since the revolution, having been created partly for purposes of defense, partly as an imitation.
>
> The concept of equality is a two-edged one here. It turns into the abdication of the individual, because the more universal any possession is, the fewer individ-

ual defenders it finds. Once people have become accustomed to the state as the sole guardian of rights and public welfare, even the *will* to decentralization no longer helps. Governments no longer entrust their provinces, cities, and other individual forces with any real matters of power, but turn over to them only those trials and tribulations which the governments absolutely can no longer cope with — something that the smaller units hardly desire. [Original emphasis.]

In those final words Burckhardt could be speaking for the mayors of America's blighted central cities. On the effect of all this upon international politics he adds:

. . . governments and peoples agree on the necessity of being powerful toward the outside. The consequences of this international situation are an immeasurable increase of militarism (since Frederick the Great there have been huge standing armies, usable at home as well as abroad) and also a colossal increase in state debts. . . .

In the end the people believe that if state power were completely in their hands they could fashion a new existence with it.

The nineteenth century ended, the Great War followed; the reactionary French novelist Céline describes his experience: "Lost in the midst of two million madmen, all of them heroes, at large and armed to the teeth! . . . sniping, plotting, flying, kneeling, digging, taking cover, wheeling, detonating, shut in on earth as in an asylum cell; intending to wreck everything in it, Germany, France, the whole world, every breathing thing; destroying, more ferocious than a pack of mad dogs and adoring their own madness."

Lost amidst madmen — powerless. Karl Jaspers, the German philosopher, in a reflection written in 1931, on the eve of the collapse of the Weimar Republic:

. . . since (even in favorable situations) the individual has no more than restricted powers of intervention, and cannot fail to recognize that the actual results of his doings depend far more upon general environing conditions than upon the aims he is trying to fulfill; since, therefore, he is made poignantly cognizant of the small extent of his sphere of influence as compared with the vast possibilities of which he is abstractly aware; and since, finally, the course of the world (which no one is satisfied with) seems to him in many ways undesirable — a feeling of powerlessness has become rife, and man tends to find himself dragged along in the wake of events which, when in a more sanguine mood, he had hoped to guide. . . . Today . . . the pride which aims at universal understanding, and the arrogance of one who regards himself as master of the world and therefore wants to mold it to his liking, knock at all doors, while their frustration arouses a feeling of terrible impotence.

Or Bede Griffiths, an English intellectual convert to Roman Catholicism in the 1930's, later a Benedictine monk:

Just as we saw in the scientific mind, with its lack of imagination, the cause of the ugliness and inhumanity of modern civilization, so we looked on law and morality, in so far as they were separated from love, as the principal cause of evil. I do not think that we should have condemned law and morality as such, any more than we condemned science and reason in themselves; but the divorce of the moral reason and conscience from instinct and passion was what we rebelled against. Love was for us in the sphere of action what imagination was in the world of thought and production. Reason without imagination and morality without love were the two great sources of evil in human life and in our own civilization in particular.

Or still more recently, after World War II, the French novelist and radically conservative essayist Georges Bernanos:

> Hasn't the time come for us to wonder if all our misfortunes don't have one common cause, if this form of civilization is not an accident, a sort of pathological phenomenon in the history of humanity? One might say that it is not machine civilization so much as it is the invasion of civilization by machines, the most serious consequence of which is to modify profoundly not only the environment in which man lives but man himself. Let us not be deceived.

Or again:

> The democracies have been decomposing too, but some decompose more quickly than others. They have been decomposing into bureaucracy, suffering from it as a diabetic does from sugar, at the expense of his own substance. In the most advanced cases, this bureaucracy itself decomposes into its most degraded form, police bureaucracy. At the end of this evolution, all that is left of the state is police.

Or to provide a coda upon these conservative themes, the contemporary American historian and philosopher of history John Lukacs: a new division has opened up, not between liberals and conservatives but "between partisans of reason and partisans of progress, between those who still see no sense in resisting the increasing mechanization of the world and those who *no longer* share these outdated ideas of Progress." *

The new radicals of the 1970's, with their assault upon

---

* On the Modern Age, Lukacs adds: "If we . . . turn to the motivating (that is, accepted and acceptable) ideas . . . we will find not only that . . . they move remarkably slowly, but also that they are painfully old. International organization, world government, disarmament, the population explosion, the administrative society, the welfare state, mass production, automation, progressive education, psychoanalysis, abstract art,

machine society, "plastic civilization," bureaucratic tyr-
anny and technocracy, the rule of greed, power aggran-
dizement, the debasement of popular culture and the
manipulation of mass culture, the "narcotizing" of the
masses while their freedom is being stolen: they could
as well be thunderers of the old European conservatism.
Just as the new prophets of a radical counter-culture give
expression to a romantic vision — a Blakean vision — of a
natural, organic world restored, which was clearly pre-
saged in the literary and esthetic movements of Europe a
half-century ago, so the political and social prophets of the
new radicalism give expression to what is, in essential
respects, a disguised conservative impulse, even a disguised reaction.

I I

But is this important? Today's is a movement of a different
time, a distinctly different spirit, a new cast of crisis. Yet
the resemblances are suggestive. We must understand that
the present unrest is novel, but not fundamentally new.
We should understand that what we today experience
may in fact be the culmination, the arrival at the point of
catalysis, of social and material forces inherent in modern
industrial society and culture, but that these factors of
dissonance and disintegration have been visible since the
beginning and have persistently been articulated, as we
see, from very different quarters.

In the beginning the reaction was mounted in the
name of the recapturable past, the organic and hier-
archical past of a preindustrial social order which in the

Greenwich Village, tubular furniture, emancipated women—they were
current, accepted, in evidence, *idées reçues* in . . . 1913."

nineteenth century was still visible outside the machine centers and the new urban conglomerates. It was, for intellectuals and for the articulate middle classes, a reaction in defense of a society of rank and responsibilities, a social order which still possessed some vitality in Europe until our own day. Thus the conservative critique possessed reference to a reality: the alternative social order was not an act of imagination but vestigially visible, part of the experience and memory of the living society.

Actually, the very fact that the alternative society was a known society contributed to the failure of European conservatism. The old order, after all, had deliberately been repudiated at a bloody cost. The strictures on the new dangers of democratic despotism made by a Burckhardt or Tocqueville, the anti-industrial esthetics of the German *Wandervögel*, or of Bede Griffiths or T. S. Eliot, could mean little to a Russian Jew emigrating to America, survivor of pogroms and Cossacks, or to a Sicilian peasant greeting the Risorgimento — or greeting Mussolini. The joys of aristocratic title may have been irresistible to the daughters — and mothers — of America's arriviste rich at the turn of the century; but even they were often willfully suppressing their own deeper knowledge that aristocracies were a relic of a past not theirs, an unsupportable, somehow fraudulent claim to put forward in the twentieth century. Lampedusa's Sicilian prince understood that he was the last of the line, "this gaunt giant now dying on a hotel balcony. For the significance of a noble family lies entirely in its traditions, that is in its vital memories; and he was the last to have any unusual memories." The prince — the "Leopard" — makes his deathbed confession: "Things should be done properly or not at all. Everyone went out, but when he was about to speak he realized he had nothing to say; he could remember some definite sins, but they seemed so petty as not to warrant bothering a worthy priest about on a hot day. Not that he felt himself innocent; but his whole life was blameworthy, not this or that single act in it; and now he no longer had time to say so."

A stoic summing up for a ruling class and social order. The conservatism of Europe in the twentieth century grasped the magnitude of what the modern world had wrecked in the lives of men, but it has also been paralyzed as a political movement by the magnitude of what also has been created by the modern world. It has been paralyzed as well by the inevitability of what is, as against what once was. Such intellectual and moral validity as conservatism possessed has been as it provided a critical stance, a detached sensibility, a place from which to weigh the consequences of actions which nonetheless had to be taken.*

In America, except in isolated enclaves of the South and New England, conservatism has been less than that;

---

* A different and more hostile judgment was provided by Benjamin Disraeli, writing in 1844: ". . . while forms and phrases are religiously cherished in order to make the semblance of a creed, the rule of practice is to bend to the passion or combination of the hour. Conservatism assumes in theory that everything established should be maintained, but adopts in practice that everything that is established is indefensible. To reconcile this theory and this practice, they produce what they call 'the best bargain,' some arrangement which has no principle and no purpose except to obtain a temporary lull of agitation, until the mind of the Conservatives, without a guide and without an aim, distracted, tempted, and bewildered, is prepared for another arrangement, equally statesmanlike with the preceding one.

"Conservatism was an attempt to carry on affairs by substituting the fulfilment of the duties of office for the performance of the functions of government, and to maintain this negative system by the mere influence of property, reputable private conduct, and what are called good connexions. Conservatism discards prescription, shrinks from principle, disavows progress; having rejected all respect for antiquity, it offers no redress for the present, and makes no preparation for the future. It is obvious that for a time, under favorable circumstances, such a confederation might succeed, but it is equally clear, that on the arrival of one of those critical conjunctures that will periodically occur in all states, it has hardly existed. America, pre-eminently, has been the liberal society, with no room for anything else. America has had its populist reactionary politics, its radical reactionaries, its racists and its persecutors of classes, elites and religions in the name of fancied absolutisms, its inquisitorial vengeance takers upon the present — the Know-Nothing movement, the American Protective League, the Palmer raiders, the anti-Communist legionnaires of the Joseph McCarthy years — but these all were rightist fanaticisms, not conservatism. What has passed for an American conservatism in the last few years, the Goldwater movement in the Republican party, the new conservative third parties arising in several states, the publicists and intellectuals grouped around the *National Review*, ordinarily is not conservative at all. It is a peculiarly American inversion of liberalism, a caricature of liberalism, an antiliberalism which, like antimatter, exists only by virtue of what it opposes. It displays the identical optimism, the same naïve historicism, the same conviction of American moral pre-eminence and mission to the world, the same ultimately materialist values as the worst of the American political liberalism it purports to despise. Robert Lifton has said: ". . . America has not only lacked a feudal social structure but has grown out of a series of specific breakdowns of feudal structures in other cultures, or else out of the piecemeal sequestering of deviant individuals and groups from every variety of larger social unit. The resulting strain upon Americans' sense of the past — our polar tendencies to deny on the one hand that any past has existed or is needed, and on the other hand to expand

and which such an unimpassioned system is even calculated ultimately to create, all power of resistance will be wanting: the barren curse of political infidelity will paralyse all action; and the Conservative Constitution will be discovered to be a Caput Mortuum."

in idealized, sometimes desperate, terms the past we possess — can hardly be argued."

Yet it is here that a tie undeniably exists between the New Populism and the existing American right. As elements in the Nixon Administration have grasped, the populist experience of the new anxieties of modern society is potentially, although as yet only potentially, mobilizable within the American rightist tradition of vengeance-taking, this paranoid political style. But such a mobilization almost certainly would ultimately fail, since the American right, this antiliberalism which passes for conservatism, has nothing real to offer a man whose anger is not simply with the liberal establishment, with an elite indifferent to his plight, but is anger, anxiety, at certain conditions of modern life itself. The American right can ultimately offer him only more unrest, more social dislocation, more political turbulence and struggle, more war.

If the American experience offered the possibility of a recapturable past, as preliberal Europe still did even in this century, then the right might have some *seriousness* about it. In Spain and Portugal forty years ago it was possible — at great human cost — to freeze the society in an archaic style and structure. But that was because these *were* preliberal states which never had gone through the nineteenth-century European intellectual revolution, transforming the outlook as well as the political power of the middle classes. In Spain and Portugal (as still is the case in much of Latin America), a landowning or professional middle class perpetuated a pre-Enlightenment social outlook, and in a time of stress allied itself with generals to impose these values upon the nation — with the superficial help of Fascist trappings (soon discarded when they lost their utility) and the Catholic social theory of corporatism (a system which perpetuated in modernized terms the old orders and guilds, and the old notions of class responsibilities and hierarchies).

In Greece today, which is another preliberal nation lacking a modern middle class, a junta of colonels is attempting to restore Orthodox Christian morality, to do away with mini-skirts and rock music, to re-establish patriotism and seemly behavior among the young — to isolate Greece not only from Communism but from the fancied corruptions which have swept the rest of Europe, to rescue it from the second half of the twentieth century. Their political and moral vision (unlike that of the young colonels of certain Middle Eastern and Asian revolutionary movements) is simply reactionary. They would like to re-create in Greece their romanticized conception of the nineteenth century's Europe *de Papa*. Theirs is a response not so much to the new anxieties affecting contemporary liberal Europe as to a nexus of the larger forces of modern history, only now belatedly affecting Greece. Their political lineage lies in an old Greek struggle between preliberal forces, traditionally grouped around the monarchy, and a republican movement whose own "liberalism" is redolent of the nineteenth century rather than the twentieth. Thus theirs is a kindred movement to Salazar's or Franco's authoritarianism, an attempt to reinstate God, duty, decorum and authority to their lost places. It is a phenomenon of those societies which the liberal political and intellectual revolutions of the mid-nineteenth century by-passed or only superficially affected, agrarian societies where the feudal social order has only relatively recently begun to break down, societies where — in Hugh Seton-Watson's terms — the premodern system of vertically imposed state power has only begun to be supplanted by the extensive horizontal relationships and interdependencies characteristic of modern society, economy and government. In short, the Greek "solution" is no solution to the new forces of the present day, but responds rather to the late arrival of the old forces of European liberalism. It still makes an appeal to the most traditional and rigid social sectors elsewhere in Europe — Italian army officers, or elements of the French or Italian aristocracies or *hautes bourgeoisies* — but it could hardly be imposed anywhere outside Balkan or Iberian Europe, and not for very much longer even there. It has nothing to say to the modern liberal West — or to the modern liberal crisis.

In today's crisis a conservative resort to the ideas, institutions and values of the past is impossible because there simply is no useful past: which is to say that it is part of the nature of the modern system that it destroys the past, the social institutions and communities of the past, and the values which sustained them. Thus the thrust of the New Populism is truly modern — as with all populisms, despite their rightist style and links, which arise from their need to oversimplify and tame a threatening new social context. The thrust of the New Populism is forward, radically reformist and in search of a new social integration — which also makes it vulnerable to that peculiarly modern phenomenon, ideological totalitarianism. *

---

* Totalitarianism must clearly be distinguished from reaction, although in popular and polemical discourse this hardly ever is done. Thus the persisting but profoundly misleading tendency to call Greece today, or Spain and Portugal under Franco and Salazar, totalitarian, when actually they are conservative or reactionary regimes for whom the epithets "despotic," "tyrannical" or "repressive" are accurate. They are not *total* in their political and moral claims — they defer to the Church, for an obvious example — nor is the power they actually exercise over the lives of their people total.

I I I

The New Populism and the New Left have this in common, which decisively sets them off from conservatism: they look forward, not back. But forward to what? The anti-intellectual New Populist hardly knows, except in negative terms. He has wrongs to be redressed, enemies — elites, establishments, interests, conspiracies — to be turned out of power. Beyond that is only a dim perception of restored national wholeness and moral rightness.

The New Left, on the other hand, is passionately articulate, intelligible. Its critique of the contemporary world may only be a reformulation of the old conservative attack, but it is truly modern in that it despises the past, furiously repudiates past as well as present. The new radicalism displaces the idealized society to the future. Instead of the old organic society of feudal orders, agricultural community, hierarchy, elites of family service and inherited tradition, it postulates a new organic society of liberated individuals, communal settlements, unrepressed impulse and spontaneous affections. Instead of the conservative attachment to landed wealth and values, the new movement would break free from the capitalist system, but also often places an extraordinary faith in the ability of that system to be automated into laborless production for all. Instead of the old conservative defense of orthodox religion against the secularism of science, the new movement proclaims the creation of "a new heaven and earth" where science and technique must "of necessity withdraw in the presence of such splendor to a subordinate and marginal status in the lives of men." And the new movement, on its margins at least, includes a revival of astrology and

137

the occult, the practice of the *Book of Changes*, macrobiotic dieting to purge the senses, and drugs to induce mystical experience and an alleged new receptivity to truth.

The new rebels realize that their goal, this transformed world, cannot be described in any very specific or material terms, only in generalities and the language of values. They rightly say, with Guevara, that a revolution makes itself. They say that their own task is to tear off the "smiling mask" from today's system, to confront and discredit it, to destroy it, and then what will follow will follow. They are the harbingers of the new world, preaching that a new dispensation will come, but not what it will be like.

With this we arrive at the second characteristic which sets them off from liberalism as well as from conservatism. Their faith in the future reveals their soaring optimism; they declare an *unreasonable* commitment to progress, a commitment which exists in paradoxical defiance of the attack they make on the old Enlightenment progressivism and Marxist historicism. Theirs is a belief in a salvationary progress which needs only to be loosed from the bonds of contemporary social stasis — the "repressive system" — in order to fulfill itself.

The difference between this new kind of rebellion and the old liberalism or socialism it despises is simply that the one denies, while the others accept, that the free future can be worse as well as better, and that to act in politics demands a *reasonable* appreciation of the consequences of action. When the American radical priest and war resister Daniel Berrigan says that the task is to "create a world anew, beginning with man himself," these words are not, as I understand Berrigan, to be regarded as rhetoric at all, but as a serious statement of his aims. If you believe in the need for no new politics but a re-created world and re-created man, then it follows that the political conditions which exist today contain little that merits scruple or discrimination. The differences that do exist shrink into insignificance by comparison with the radiant world and new man to be called into being.

Thus the radical can reasonably describe as "Fascist" contemporary France or Britain or America, or the liberal political system as such. The differences between Hitler's Germany with its death camps, and America with its Vietnamese war but also with its seething controversies and open politics, or between Nazism and Gaullist France with its controlled state television and authoritarian traits, or between Nazism and a British government which sells arms to South Africa, become insignificant. All of these political regimes are simply manifestations — more or less vicious — of an Old Order about to be replaced by the New. Against this is the argument represented by a man such as Walter Laqueur, who indignantly calls "absurd" the New Left's indiscriminate lumping together of Dachau with the repression of Black Panthers, or their comparison of the Hitlerian extermination of Jews, Poles and Gypsies, and Nazism's ambition to repopulate Slavic Europe with "Nordic-Phalian-Germanic blood," * with America's war policy in Indochina. Laqueur calls this radical position the result of a "lack of historical perspective so monumental as to make rational discourse impossible." He is of course

---

* Heinrich Himmler, who added: "It is . . . in the East that the decision lies; here must the Russian enemy, this people numbering two hundred million Russians, be destroyed on the battlefield, and one by one they must be made to bleed to death . . . Either they must be deported and used as labor in Germany for Germany, or they will just die in battle." This, like the genocide of the Jews, was state policy, unlike the ambition expressed by U.S. Air Force General Curtis LeMay to bomb North Vietnam "back to the stone age."

right, but for the wrong reason. The intellectually serious radical understands that there is a difference between Adolf Hitler or Heinrich Himmler and Richard Nixon or John Mitchell (or Lyndon Johnson or Ramsey Clark); his argument is simply that the differences are less important than that all these men represent, and function within, a corrupt modern order of politics and social existence that needs not to be reformed within its own terms of value but to be rooted out and replaced with a new man and a new order of things. In the lapidary words of one of the French student demands of 1968: Imagination Seizes Power.

I V

Daniel Bell declared a decade ago that we had reached "the end of ideology" because a pragmatic appreciation of social and political issues has supplanted the usefulness of ideology. His judgment might better be reformulated today to say that we are at the end of ideology because the ideologies we possess — without losing their power over the human imagination — have cut themselves loose from real possibility and real reference. Conservatism has been outmoded because today's society, with its velocity of change, puts to it problems which it cannot solve. The conservative "perennial philosophy" or "public philosophy" has been destroyed — as Hans Morgenthau has put it in a critique of Walter Lippmann — "by the modern conditions and problems of life which the public philosophy, as it has come down to us, is unable to reflect and solve. . . . [It] has not only been the reflection of the objective standards of politics, but it has also been a political ideology, and predominately an ideology of the status quo.

In other words, the existing political order was identified with the objective and rational order."

The new ideologues on the radical left, confronting the dilemma of the liberal and Marxist "success" we have already examined, have launched themselves into the realm of imagination. They postulate solutions which require a transformation of man himself — as they concede, or indeed eagerly proclaim. Because they also intuitively grasp the dimensions of what they are demanding, they are driven, on the one side, to violence, and on the other to a spurious mysticism. They indulge, at worst, in a kind of magical thinking which, at its own worst, predisposes toward an organized political irrationalism which would be of an unprecedented scale and quality (inevitably so, since great magic and a blinding act of will would be necessary to overcome the perceptions and habits of two centuries of scientific culture in the West). At best their radical criticisms and witness testify — poignantly, sometimes desperately — to the present anguish felt by political men. But they have no more real power to change our condition for the better than the outmoded right.

If we draw back from these proto-totalitarian ideologies, we are left with an inchoate body of reform movements and impulses which nonetheless accept the political world as it is, the exigencies of the present, the responsibilities — ambiguous but profound — of action in a world where men bleed, feel grief, brutalize and are brutalized. We are left with the world of *political* possibilities, but not transcendent ones. We are left with flaw and discordance, with men as moral actors in a web of interactions, and with a need to acknowledge that salvation, redemption, transformed human sensibility, are not political commodities.

Here the true line must be drawn today, between those political men, those reformers, who are *serious* and those who are not. It is not a line which runs between the right and the left. We perhaps need to abandon this language of left and right as a source of confusion. Beginning with the modern political age, in France's revolutionary parliaments, it has perhaps served its historical function. We need a postliberal politics, freed from the intellectual inheritance of the old parties and the old ideologies. But it will have to be a reasonable politics, even if at the same time we admit the limits of reason. Without reason we are cast loose in the maze. There is no political freedom without intelligence, and today intelligence itself is in need of defense.

CHAPTER VII

The Problem
of Liberal Reform

We are faced here with the problem which has never ceased to perplex mankind — the question of the very legitimacy of politics. Its utter vagueness and elusive character, the mixture of abstract principle and crass ambition, of objective goals and sheer histrionics, of rational argument and squalid bamboozling; its seeming remoteness from the concrete, measurable, and truly necessary things, all this leads to the despairing conclusion that whatever the politicians, men of no particular training, ultimately dilettanti, say or do is but a mask and pretence for the will to power, power for its own sake.

— J. L. Talmon

I

THE CONTENTION of this book is that the crisis of liberal politics is great, not small. The liberal political order has been an astonishing human accomplishment, providing institutions within which men have lived with unprecedented individual freedom and fulfillment. But it constantly is in jeopardy, endangered not least by the tensions set up by its own accomplishment of freedom. It is a provisional order. It could fail. Today it is seriously threatened. To save it is a worthwhile undertaking, but constantly hard, not easy.

The individuals who can save it are those who accept its intellectual assumptions of rational inquiry and intellectual exchange, its political assumptions of pragmatic change and majority persuasion and decision. The terrorist and the millenarian radical are necessarily excluded, even though the emotional power and impetus of radicalism are to be taken into account as a political force. But the millenarian has no *reform* to offer: he acts out, in his own life, the plight of the society, playing an exemplary role, without contributing himself to society.

The reformer who is relevant to our crisis must accept what *is* in the world, and deal in terms of attainable and intelligent change. What society is, is the outcome of what society has been: the whole creative but ravaging experience of modern civilization. To rail against it or try to elude its constraints is a politically inconsequential act. The radical's redemptive future is *possible,* one possibility in a universe of possibilities. But he is politically inconsequential because he has no efficacious way of taking us where he wants to go. When the objective is conceived in no better terms than a generalized social redemption to arise out of catastrophe (a catastrophe which it is an allegedly revolutionary act to bring about), then he does not deserve attention. The man of the right excludes himself from attention when he makes an equivalent commitment to evasion, as in the case of the naïve populisms, or to a politics of vengeance-taking, or to a restoration of the unrestorable, of the time-destroyed. We are left, then, with the despised moderates, the men who are willing to commit themselves to reason, even if they understand, as some of them do, that this too is an "absurd" commitment.

We are left with the piecemeal and the pragmatic reforms, the halting reforms, weak and unsatisfactory. We are left to discriminate among the versions of reform which today are offered us. But if, as I argue, the crisis is a major one, we must ask for reform on a major scale, a radical willingness to re-examine liberal structures. There has been too little of this. The dismaying fact about our present situation is that so little thought has been devoted to the real and practical changes which could be made in our ordering of political and economic power to the service of individual men.

I I

The most influential of today's liberal reformers of liberalism are those who still believe that our existing institutions and systems falter simply because they are not yet perfected. They say that we have hardly begun to understand how to manage our economy and society. They say that our administrative and managerial systems still are victims of the inefficiency and ignorance of the past. Our knowledge of society is actually small, but potentially it is very large. Our present methodologies of research, our analyses of our social systems and their potentialities, our ultimate power of institutional reform, are in their infancy. We are not rational enough: we have not begun to make use of technology and the resources of the social sciences to perfect our administration of society. We need more of what we already have.

These reformers, essentially technocratic, possess an intensified, heightened faith in rationalism, in a science of society able to accomplish in its area what pure science itself has accomplished in mastering material forces. Theirs is also a distinctly dated faith, a phenomenon of the years between the 1940's and the 1960's, innocent of the doubts that have come to infect science itself. In its American manifestations — and for the most part the modern technocracy has reached a kind of perfection as an American academic movement — it is too often naïve or credulous, assiduously quantifying and submitting to numerical analysis matters whose essential distinguishing characteristics are qualitative and volitional. It is also, typically, a complacent outlook: its answer to the troubles of the present is simply that we have not done well enough all of the things we are already doing.*

Moreover, that a genuinely technocratic society would be liberal is open to doubt. Not only is the power

---

* It also includes a tendency to dismiss the present troubles of liberal society as the fault of the complainers: middle-class guilt, intellectual utopianism, permissive child rearing, are the causes of our crisis. The society is held to be healthy; the diagnosticians are deluded and are producing a fit of anxiety in the hapless patient as they debate radical surgery.

centralization in a technocratic ordering of society very great, but the technocratic impulse is in considerable degree that of "guardianship" by a putatively well-disposed elite. That elite relies upon knowledge which, as Daniel Bell has optimistically argued, would be sought "in a disinterested way." But as Hannah Arendt comments, disinterestedness is possible only so long as the scientists and technologists do not rule (and it is a theoretical possibility even then, since we know that politically active scientists and technical men are in fact no less biased or partisan in judgment than anyone else, and to the extent that they are less conscious of their partisanship and preconceptions they are the more dangerous). Miss Arendt adds: "What grounds are there for supposing that the resentment against a meritocracy, whose rule is exclusively based in 'natural' gifts, that is, on brain-power, will be no more dangerous, no more violent, than the resentment of earlier oppressed groups who at least had the consolation that their condition was caused by no 'fault' of their own? Is it not plausible to assume that this resentment will harbor all the murderous traits of a racial antagonism . . . inasmuch as it too will concern natural data which cannot be changed . . . ? [S]ince in such a constellation the numerical power of the disadvantaged will be overwhelming and social mobility almost nil, is it not likely that the danger of demagogues, of popular leaders, will be so great that the meritocracy will be forced into tyrannies and despotism?"

Nor is there any particular reason to think that the "guardians" in such a system would be our best men. Those who seem most drawn toward the idea of technocratic reform and rule are usually not scientists but ambitious members of the "soft" academic disciplines; they may, like Zbigniew Brzezinski, prophesy a "superculture" created by "organization-oriented, application-minded intellectuals," but this kind of thing can hardly be taken seriously, except as an inadvertent warning. Even the most fatuously complacent of the old despots and oligarchs of Western history never promised a "superculture" as reward for their installation in power.

Nonetheless, certain forms of technocratic reform are necessary. In a wide range of the administrative and organizational functions of our society things will only be done better through professional analysis and reform. The analysis of public administration, management, the judiciary, is indispensable to reform. But what the technocrats as a class are reluctant to concede is that they and their practices are also implicated in the crisis. The bureaucratization of our society, its notorious computerization and "plasticization," has been the work of technocrats and the social scientists. Yet we are left with the technocrats to cure it if they can. How to administer a very large and complex society and economy competently is one of the formidable *professional* as well as social issues of our times, and it cannot be made to disappear with vague invocations of popular participation, or rendered a nonproblem through Luddite assaults upon the sublimely stupid computer. We are left, at this level of reform — which is an elementary level — with a series of technical and organizational problems for which professional solutions must be found.

There is another emphasis to be found within this essentially optimistic and rationalist or technocratic class of analysts and reformers. They often place a very high level of confidence in GNP growth as a solvent of social tensions and social conflict. The argument against this is not quite so simple as sometimes made out by John Kenneth Galbraith and those others who advocate a "zero rate of growth," although Galbraith's charge that crude GNP growth obscures or ignores the question of the social value of goods is both accurate and important. In all of the Western countries the "strong and persuasive industries" grow, whatever the social worth of their products, while the "backward and unpersuasive industries" — which in America include housing and public transport — function poorly. Thus the private affluence amidst public squalor of Galbraith's famous thesis.

But one of the redeeming accomplishments of liberal society has been the creation of general, although far from universal, material well-being, and this has been the outcome of "crude" industrial expansion, the free market, and a fairly undiscriminating governmental stimulation of growth. The result has been critically important to the mass of individuals in Western society whose experience in recent times has been of a fairly steadily improving standard of living. It is easy for Puritans (usually Puritans from privileged backgrounds) to disparage the lives of newly affluent workers and clerks — their barbecues and boats in the United States, their cults of automobile and telly in Britain, their increasingly "Americanized" tastes on the Continent — but this ordinarily reflects a moralizing paternalism which hardly deserves to be taken seriously. Middle-class intellectuals, anyway, are nearly always astounded, even scandalized, to learn what ordinary lives are like. In fact, life in a house of one's own, with kitchen and laundry appliances, a car, a wading pool for the children, is a good life, and if Western society can lift its poverty-stricken into such a life, it will have done humanity a service. Can it be done in the future without the dynamisms of "crude" expansion; or could these expectations of the masses be gratified with programs of economic redistribution? Whether ordinary people would accept more leisure in place of more money, better social services and public amenities in place of the goods and wages of general economic expansion — if the productive economy itself is capable of functioning effectively at some stabilized level without the growth-expansion motive — is not so easy to say. One suspects that the ordinary man wants it all: better pay *and* better social accomplishment in the public sector. One also suspects that the zero-growth philosophy, convincing as it is on some grounds, notably the environmental, includes a very wide margin of uncertainty about its real social consequences.

Money is important to this general class of reformers in another way, not only as social solvent but often as a methodology of reform. They concede that there are limits to what money can do, but they also contend that the importance of what money can do dwarfs what it can't. They argue, often correctly, that to allocate funds to solving a problem is the biggest single step in the solution, since money means that men and resources will be put to work, and even if much or most of the effort is wasted, the chance of finding a solution through waste and trial and error is considerably greater than through any narrow analytic effort. This argument is essentially that of the engineer, and is reinforced by the experience of defense science and engineering in the United States. With scientific and technological problems the scale of expenditure usually is reflected in a proportionate increase in the chances of solution. Work on a series of hypotheses, research on a major scale into a variety of approaches to a problem, more often than not prove to be the true mother of invention. You can force-feed progress in technology, and less conclusively, in science.

The argument is not clearly transferable to social expenditure. Aside from the larger question of goals — simple in science, where the problem defines the solution, but complex and open in social matters — there is the problem of consequences. Social action has consequences for people. The expenditure is on human institutions and arrangements, not objects of technology which can be discarded if they don't work. The clearest example here is the poverty program expenditures of the Johnson Administration in the United States in the 1960's, which were generous, eclectic in approach and very ambitious — trying almost any line of solution which seemed promising. While there were successes in these programs, the failures also were given life in institutions and enterprises which could not easily be discarded. There were irreversible consequences. Thus critics of the poverty programs could later assert that sectors of the American poor were mobilized and politicized but then denied constructive reforms, or that power, in the form of money, was irresponsibly delivered over to arbitrarily selected groups and individuals among the poor, to the disadvantage or disservice of the poor as a whole. But the deeds were done; the outcome was not easily to be changed.

In the United States there emerged a widespread and not wholly unjustified conviction that the generous and high-minded social programs of the late 1960's made the American social crisis worse rather than better. And they did make things worse to the extent that they inspired or underwrote expectations which could not be fulfilled. A political activism among the poor awakened them from despair but immediately put them into disastrous collisions with other power interests; a *dramatization* of the American inner-city and racial tensions was accomplished which was without a peaceful resolution. In this case funds spent without a close analysis of how or why they were to be spent had some success but proved not to be the problem solvent which money has provided in technology and engineering.

Nonetheless, there is a real importance to money allocations as a signal of political valuations and public attention. The scale of the American social investment in the late 1960's demonstrated a public will to social reform even as the continued and overwhelming predominance of military investment perpetuated an earlier scale of public valuations, still embedded in the belief and practice of the government establishment. The fact that an enlarged social investment produced contradictory results (to say nothing of the disquiet felt over the intractability of military budgets) intensified and dramatized a public frustration born of larger causes. It compounded the new public anxieties over powerlessness-amidst-power, but it also made clear one simple cause for anxiety: the government's intellectual incompetence in dealing with important areas of social responsibility and public effort.

I I I

The technologists and social scientists' approach to our problems, then, is limited but important in its own terms. Its limitation is that the maldeployment and malfunction of technique are part of the problem; its strength is that administrative reform in government, the reform of bureaucracy, the improvement of economic management, the control of technocratic innovation, all must be given professional, technocratic remedy.

That is, there are crucial areas of contemporary social, political and economic management where abuses exist which are directly and clearly remediable. These abuses are now factors in creating the anxieties lying behind the liberal crisis. There is the question of doing justice, a fundamental and indispensable function of government. Today, only 12 percent of all reported major crimes are followed by arrests, and of these, only half end in convictions. The significance of the statistics available in these matters is arguable, since it is not clear that reported crime very accurately corresponds to actual crime in society, and some of the crimes which are reported might better be placed in other classifications of social disorder or distress. Nonetheless, the general significance of the situation is clear enough: from the viewpoint of victims, and of the ordinary citizen who wishes to live in a community where civil order and safety are maintained, justice is not being done. The same judgment can be made for those who are arrested and accused of crime. In the larger American cities the delay between arrest and trial is commonly two years. This is an unconscionable affront to the principle and constitutional requirement that an accused man be given a prompt trial. A worse delay ordinarily exists in civil disputes, and for the ordinary man, who has neither the funds, access to legal talent — nor life expectancy — of the corporation, placing a civil suit is usually an exercise in frustration.

This is true with respect to the administrative legislation governing the functions of our society — legislation which too often is evaded or ignored by the privileged, unenforced by the state, leaving the individual a seemingly powerless victim of an institutionalized cynicism he cannot affect. This is notoriously true in bureaucracy-choked Italy, where only the stupid and the poor pay taxes to scale, and true but less so in recent years in France. It is increasingly true of the United States, where the charge that "there is no longer a functioning system of law" can plausibly be made by a moderate commentator (Tom Wicker of the *New York Times*, in support of views expressed by Adam Walinsky):

> Defrauded consumers, home owners with uncollected garbage, commuters who cannot get to work, persons awaiting trial in impossibly crowded courts, students in institutions that do not teach, pedestrians breathing air noxious with pollution, utility users unable to get adequate service from protected monopolies, victims of the thousands of crimes that annually go unsolved, motorists in massive traffic jams — all are victims either of irrelevant law, lack of law, unworkable law, unenforced law, corruption, official disinterest or official disability. In this real and practical sense, for all these millions of people, "there is no law."

The causes include undermanned and maladministered or inadequate administrative agencies, police departments and regulatory bodies, an insufficient number and inadequate funding of courts, a variety of legislative and administrative impediments: illogical jurisdictions, the assignment to criminal courts of matters which ought to be in the civil jurisdiction, and to the civil courts of matters which deserve administrative handling, arbitration or referee procedures; the criminal prosecution of certain victimless offenses, and above all, the lack of a real will to do justice. All of this is widely recognized, as are the means to reform. The obstacles are money and the lack of a decision to reform. But to make it possible for the courts to do justice there is a simple first step: spend the money necessary to provide enough courts.

Even the famous issue of law and order in the streets has belatedly come to be understood to express an absolutely fundamental civic demand: felt by citizens of all classes and races, perhaps most keenly of all by the poor, who typically are the most numerous victims both of crime and of police abuses. Again there is a simple solution, an indispensable and necessary solution, if not a comprehensive one. It is to put more and better-trained, better-commanded police on the streets. No doubt much can be done to improve the community's relationship with the police and civil control of the police, and no doubt much can be done to change and improve the police forces themselves. But the first step in solving the problem is to have enough police and to pay them well enough so that talented and able men will remain in police service. Again it is necessary to spend money.

To provide other social services whose present deterioration so affects the morale of society, money is the fundamental and indispensable requirement. To have clean streets, clean parks, good medical services for all the population, good housing, pensions, good public transportation, neither research nor further analysis of the situation is needed. There is no mystery about how to do these things. You spend money. You may spend it well or badly, and no doubt analysis of the problems will help you spend it well, but the most important decision is to hire and properly pay street cleaners, trash collectors, transportation workers and medical technicians, orderlies and doctors. It is to devote funds to building clinics, health centers, houses and apartments, and rebuilding subways and railroads. In much of Europe this is already done on an adequate, and often on a generous, scale. In the United States it is not. The money is denied these services because in the past the valuation placed on them by the politically articulate sector of the population was low. Today the public valuation is quite high, but not yet sufficiently high to compel the government to collect new taxes or to redirect funds from other sectors. This reluctance to redeploy funds is culpable, and it is as much a consequence of the inertia of civil service bureaucracy and of the bureaucratic intelligence as it is a result of the moral and intellectual investments of the elected government. These conditions can be changed if there is a will to change. For the United States to devote between $60 billion and $100 billion annually, directly or indirectly, to the military (half of the federal budget) may or may not express the public will — it is highly doubtful that it does today.* To spend this amount and at the same time refuse to increase taxes for other expenditures when the needs of the social sector are

---

* The case for redirecting military expenditures and reducing the size and influence of the "military-industrial complex" in America has been argued extensively and well by other writers. I will add only this: The present size of the American military establishment had its origins in real threats, not fancied ones, even though the reality has become terribly entangled in America's own ideology and discreditable fears. The Soviet Union is an unstable society today and a highly militarized one, to say nothing of an ideologically hostile state. Great issues continue to divide nations, and war remains a resort of state power. What has happened in America is a vastly *disproportionate* military growth: not only disproportionate to the real utility of the kinds of force we possess in the variety of seriously imaginable political contexts but disproportionate to the inner needs of American society. Indeed, the size of American military expenditure has been profoundly corrupting to the military forces themselves, whose own competence and integrity today are in great doubt. To reduce military spending no doubt involves certain calculable risks: those risks are trivial by comparison to the inner disintegration and moral malaise of American society. Moreover, our present forces are designed to serve a huge mission of world-wide intervention — a misconceived policy in the past, irrelevant to the real needs of the future.

so acute, is an instance of liberal government's intellectual and moral bankruptcy.

I V

A recovery of confidence is possible within the existing liberal structure, or at least a provisional recapturing of national morale based on a series of practical reforms, when these reforms are designed and sustained by a leadership with confidence in itself and knowledge of its goals. In the 1960's France successfully rebuilt its political society in the aftermath of a deep crisis of war and colonial policy. The new anxieties of modern society were implicated in this crisis, and it was deepened by failures of the party system and parliamentary functioning. The Gaullist recovery, in the end, also produced the most romantic of the modern rebellions, the Paris Spring of 1968. But the Gaullist experience is worth attention.

It was, to begin with, national and *nationalist* in its appeal. The Gaullist movement was deliberately classless, hostile to the old communal and class divisions of French society, the *régime des partis*. It successfully cut across the old established constituencies of the parties, incorporating voters from all of them. The Gaullist party was never, quite, classifiable in terms of the traditional right and left. Ordinarily called rightist, it nevertheless had little in common with the old French right, where it found its most implacable opponents. The right hated De Gaulle; the left, officially hostile, never quite overcame its ambivalence.

Gaullism was antiparliamentarian, contemptuous of the "interest group politics" of the Chamber of Deputies, yet at the same time it was democratic — committed to

republican government (De Gaulle saved the Republic
twice) — and in the end the general was willing to depart
when the electorate rejected him. His style was authoritarian but ultimately subordinated to the popular will. He
made use of television and referendums to create a kind of
dialogue between the leader and his people, symbolically
discarding the intervening apparatus of representation
and bureaucracy. This had an obviously spurious or illu-
sory quality to it, as well as totalitarian antecedents, but it
responded to a popular perception of inaccessible mechanism of power, of political anonymity and victimization. At the same time Gaullism's undogmatic willingness
to experiment with structural reforms in French society,
in the university and school systems (belatedly, but
imaginatively), in worker "participation," its meritocracy,
all contributed to a quality of responsiveness, of attentive-
ness to the popular will. French history and national identity were made powerful use of in order to reassert a special
and important meaning to French citizenship, and this in
some degree responded to popular anxieties of moral dislocation in modern society, of political alienation and loss
of assured identity.

The self-conscious modernism of Gaullism was an important factor addressing the new anxieties in French
society. The leaders who emerged as De Gaulle's lieuten-
ants represented new elements in France's changing
society. Georges Pompidou, of peasant stock but an intellectual, patron of the arts, self-made international financial
executive, represented a meritocracy, a new class of undogmatic and sophisticated French managers and political
men. The young managers of French technocracy and
capitalist enterprise joined De Gaulle, themselves the
directors of an economy pragmatically divided between

private and public sectors, highly competitive in world markets, sustained by a sophisticated state planning system.

The new capitalism and industry of France in 1958, the soaring economy (like the nuclear strike force), were not De Gaulle's creations but the result of developments and decisions under the Fourth Republic. But the Gaullists capitalized on France's economic modernization and the Common Market, exploited and developed it (even though De Gaulle's own notorious indifference to the "commissariat" contributed to his economic and social troubles in 1968). Under Gaullism, France, in its economy, industry and technology, was well served by competent men, and was in the vanguard of Europe and the West, and this had much to do with the new self-confidence and sense of meaningful enterprise of the French people.

Besides economic and technological competence, Gaullism was politically competent. The dreadful, draining crises of Algeria and of France's military-civil conflict, for so long unsolved, were ruthlessly cauterized and cured. De Gaulle disciplined the army, freed Algeria, suppressed military mutiny and civil uprising, brought back the Algerian French and integrated them into the metropolitan society, transformed the remaining French empire into a voluntary association, and asserted an independent European and world policy. There was evident in all of this the supreme political capacity — the ability to decide, to act, and to be done with it: to calculate and to minimize the costs of action, to discard failures and to reverse unprofitable policies.

The new foreign policy was nationalist, or internationalist within terms which exploited France's sense of historical identity — as in the 1950 proposal that France and West Germany rebuild (as De Gaulle put it) "on a modern basis, that is economically, socially, strategically, and culturally, the Charlemagne Empire." The symbols of national community and history were put to moral use among Frenchmen, who suffered, among other afflictions, a loss of confidence in their nation, and indeed in the political culture of liberal Europe. French foreign policy was classically concerned with the national interest, but explicitly acknowledged — in Europe, in aid to the ex-colonies — a certain "obligation to history."

Much could also be said in criticism of Gaullism, even though it constitutes, on balance, a most imposing political achievement, a political legacy to France which history will honor. But with respect to the new political forces of our own day, Gaullism was most striking for its sensitivity of response to the modern social situation as well as to the particular French conditions of the 1950's and 1960's. There was a series of elements in Gaullism which directly responded to the new popular anxieties of liberal society.

The experience was also one which is not easily translated to another nation and another time. Traces of the Gaullist rhetoric, the Gaullist ambition, can be found among the new conservative politicians of Germany, Britain, even among the technocratic moralists of Opus Dei in Spain, but these men and movements ordinarily are without De Gaulle's intelligence and his power to appeal to the left. No Malraux, no ex-Communist *résistant*, commits himself to the German CDU, or to Enoch Powell in Great Britain (although Powell, an intellectual populist, makes an appeal to the British workingman; but Powell's appeal is to impulses of racial exclusiveness, not to idealism).

The Gaullist episode nonetheless is one from which the

other liberal societies can learn. When the towering personality of De Gaulle himself and his wartime inheritance are disregarded, the relevant lessons seem twofold: to be *competent,* and to grasp the importance, in an age of isolation and lost identity, of *national community.*

V

At a second level of reform we confront the question of basic changes in the structure of the liberal system. Here are socialists still able to believe that a larger involvement of government in industrial ownership and management will make society more humane, and a few liberal reformers who believe that changes in the parliamentary system or (in the American case) in the system of delegating governmental authority could make an important difference in the lives of people.

The trouble with the socialist remedy, as we have seen, is that it recommends more of the same measures which have decisively contributed to creating the society we already have in Britain, Sweden, Germany and the United States. John Mander, a British socialist commentator, makes an ostensibly optimistic assessment of socialism's future by saying that it will, in Europe at least (he foresees, undoubtedly accurately, a new period of American political isolation from Europe), "play an increasingly important role" — but as a "civilizing influence" on Western society. That may be so, and certainly social democracy can be seen historically as a "civilizing" movement, altering the perceptions and programs of other parties and of Western society as a whole. But so modest an accomplishment is hardly that aspired to by the socialist of the past. Nor is such a view of the future likely to set the blood pounding among the disconsolate youth and alienated workers of America or Italy or Germany. The socialists today simply no longer have the confidence of their own fundamental and traditional programs: nationalization, radical redistribution of wealth, planned central direction of society. These have been tried and have not worked as expected; they have been tried and the people were bored, unconvinced. As a result the socialist movement has fallen back to a role wholly within the established terms of liberal society — the "civilizing" role indeed, not to be despised but no remedy for the crisis of our times.

Within the American debate, significant proposals have been made about changing the way in which Congress functions or the President is elected, or, as we will see, the way in which governmental power is employed, but none offers a wholly convincing prospect for altering either the *competence* of American government, or the *quality* of politics and society. They again demonstrate that for all the contemporary calls for change, the new fashionableness of a radical vocabulary and posture, very little serious thought has yet been given to how the liberal political system and economy can be reformed.

Certain structural changes in the American system are being dictated by events. The capitalist system itself is discarding sectors to public control, as in the aerospace industries and the railroads. A new generation of laws regulating consumer standards and environmental pollution will make an important change in the social accountability of the private sector. The entire system of economic regulation is being challenged in the course of a more general attack upon the "interest-group liberalism" of the New Deal and subsequent years, an attack which alleges that power has been delegated to private interests without imposing serious standards of social performance and accountability.

Certain major structural changes have been suggested in what amount to our two most serious recent analyses of Federal reform. Peter F. Drucker has proposed that the central government discard a whole series of functions which could be carried out by the private sector or by semi-autonomous public agencies on the models of the Tennessee Valley Authority in the United States or the British Broadcasting Corporation. He contends that modern government is distinguished by impotence rather than power, that government bureaucracies are poorly qualified to administer huge social undertakings, and indeed that modern government's vast functions have been attached to it largely by historical accident. The central government, he says, should serve primarily to make policy, to manage rather than to administer.

A related approach to the same problems of structural efficiency and accountability in government is Theodore Lowi's. Lowi, of the University of Chicago, contends that the American liberal government since the New Deal has delegated power to agencies and interest groups with a generalized injunction to them to discover their own solutions and regulate themselves. The government thus has defaulted on its obligation to establish what the standards should be, to *govern*. In the economy these regulatory agencies have become allies of those they regulate, with fundamental interests in common which are not those of the community as a whole, largely determining their own standards of conduct. There has been an equivalent process in political matters. Thus in the case of the poverty programs of the 1960's, not only was power delegated to community action groups, ad-hoc local bodies, newly created agencies, but also the responsibility for finding solutions. Therefore, Lowi argues, the government has created a system for lending its own authority to "private decisions reached by a process dimly specified in the statute." It follows that the government functions by bargaining with groups of its own creation which have a fundamental interest in avoiding general rules and evading public accountability.

Lowi insists that the duty of government is to set explicit public standards and rules, and to see that they are carried out by means of a reformed civil service which is given positive law to execute and standards to enforce in the courts. Power is to be used, not delegated. He does not address the Drucker proposals, but it would appear that his and Drucker's plans envisage much the same policymaking role for government itself. How autonomous would Drucker's new public corporations or agencies actually be? Autonomy in action and in setting standards of internal efficiency is one thing, as in the case of the postal service, but would the new agencies have clear mandates of public service as well as explicit standards of public accountability? Without that, a devolution of public services to the private or semiprivate sector would create an intolerable conflict between the self-validating agency and the public interest.

V I

There are levels of liberal government today where the structures of popular access to power are still vital, and here there is much controversy but no political anomie. The local levels of government, below that of the major cities, still function well. The links between people and power are short and tight. Officials are accessible and accountable to public opinion. Referendums and town meetings, council and school-board elections, are vivaciously debated and hotly contested. The issues directly affect people's lives.

In the larger centers (and in the United States, in state government), a process of centralization has taken place over the last half-century which originated in the effort to make government more rational and more efficient, and to reform specific abuses. Local governments were consolidated or annexed to larger metropolitan units. Power was translated to higher levels in order to rationalize services and administration, and to extend the tax base and equalize tax burdens. New representative bodies were introduced, as between the town meeting of the New England village (impractical above a certain level of population) and town administration, but villages and towns also were abolished by incorporation into larger units. The motive was reform; the results have included an important transformation of the active constituency of the enlarged government bodies, from individuals to those groups of individuals (and more often those special interest groups) who organized themselves in sufficient numbers and with sufficient funds to make their voice heard.

It is, of course, alluring to exalt local democracy in the absence of it, to romanticize a form of government which originated in very small rural communities, and to look nostalgically at those communities as exemplifying a lost republican integrity. In fact, the political virtues of those communities were very mixed, and corruption, coercion and the tyrannization of minorities (Negroes in the American South, immigrant communities in the North and West) have been traits impartially distributed among nearly all levels of government. The principle of decentralized power has in it as much myth as the principle of "guardianship" by a high-minded professional, intellectual or social elite — the idea which has been the unspoken assumption behind many of the Fabian and technocratic centralizing reforms of government.

Yet there is a neglected principle of reform which is relevant today. Reform constantly needs to be done over. There is merit in change for the sake of change. If centralization was a reform movement relevant to the liberal states during the first half of this century (as well as an imperative of the national consolidations of the nineteenth century), it is no contradiction but an inevitability that decentralization becomes the reform impulse of the present day. Power in any large social unit can take only two organizational forms, centralized or decentralized, and reform — in business management, in bureaucracies, in industrial and military organizations — amounts to an oscillation from one to the other. The change itself amounts to a reform. An organization has a life span of efficiency: efficiency is renewed simply by change itself. But in political organization this alternation of forms has not, ordinarily, taken place. Centralization of power has been a largely uninterrupted process spurred on by external threats to the nation, by wars, by the technocratic impulse to rationalize power, and by the simple impulse of established authority to aggrandize power.

In any decentralization of power there will be costs, and losses. Moreover, there are clear limits to any decentralization of political power in modern conditions. The number and importance of the functions which need to be carried out for society as a whole are far beyond what they have ever been before. Yet the intuition that the time has come for decentralization is very widely felt. In the United States it provided the elusive, hazily articulated theme of the McCarthy presidential campaign of 1968. It was a stated theme — the "New Federalism" — of the Nixon campaign that same year. It has been embraced by publicists of the liberal wing of the Democratic party, in different ways, usually quite tentative, by such men as Richard Goodwin and Arthur Schlesinger, Jr. It is an ancient theme of the right — and indeed "states' rights" is the conservatives' traditional issue, even if it often has served chiefly to perpetuate racial discrimination in the local law and custom of the South. Decentralization is a new reform platform in West European politics. The idea is in the air.

In France, decentralization was one in a series of "revolutionary" demands by the student rebels of 1968, and it evoked a certain serious response from the government — which, not surprisingly, has found it neither easy to carry out nor a panacea. It is being seriously attempted in Italy with the creation of a series of new regional political units. Europe's experiments with political decentralization are far more ambitious than America's for all of America's inheritance of republican rhetoric, of regard for local government as (in Jefferson's words) "the wisest invention ever devised by the best wit of man for the perfect exercise of self-government."* Yet even in Europe the

* The establishment of ten "federal regions" in the United States in 1969 involved a degree of decentralization within the five federal agencies which were affected, but was essentially an administrative reform rather than a true devolution or decentralization of power — which is to say of popular control over government. The same judgment must be made of

issues of decentralization have only begun to be addressed, while in America discussion remains, for the most part, at the level of platitude, generalization and aspiration. Yet the most profound administrative and organizational problems exist; they are not insoluble, but they involve great issues of democratic political society. There is intellectual and practical work to be done here which could transform the quality of liberal politics. The work has hardly been begun, and that is exactly the problem.

If I write of decentralized power with this emphasis it is not because it can, in itself, provide a resolution to all of our difficulties and anxieties. The limit to what it can accomplish is fairly clear; the centralizing imperative is powerful in both modern government and economy. The more important anxieties of our day, the moral anxieties, will not directly be ended by any devolution of power. To restore competence in the function of government as it already exists is critically important, of more immediate importance than decentralization. Moreover, the morale of liberal society, the *legitimacy* of liberal government, the conviction of moral value and identity among citizens, all will be vitally affected by matters to which the next chapter is addressed. But *powerlessness*, the real powerlessness and political impotence of individuals in matters vitally affecting their lives, can be remedied. In a whole series of matters directly touching upon people's lives, power can be restored. Power over schools, over the police, over social services and social amenities, power within the

the Nixon Administration's proposal in January 1971 for sharing federal revenue with states and local governments. The plan itself deserved support; money is indispensable to serious renewal of the lower levels of government. But without an equivalent transfer of real power to the lower levels, a revitalization of democratic control at those levels, the reforms will be minor. The new Italian and French decentralization programs do transfer power.

national parties — all can be restored to citizens who do not now possess it, or who possess it only through broken or choked channels of representation and bureaucratic organization.

If the people of an American town of 10,000 population can directly control their schools, there is no serious reason why a community of equivalent size in an urban center cannot and should not do so. The objections are habitual and bureaucratic; they have to do with the established distribution of tax monies and the career structure of the teachers. These problems can be solved. The objections have to do with the fear in the larger community that the 10,000 will not run their schools in the way the larger community wants. This is the argument of paternalism (and sometimes of racism) — or of vested interest. Within the limits of accreditation and civil law, including the laws requiring racial impartiality, the 10,000 deserve to run their schools with the same autonomy that the rural or suburban community enjoys (or, through the voucher system, be given the means to support whatever private schools they want, under the same general public limitations).

Within the limits of certain central, metropolitan functions and with the support of a central tax base with a per-capita apportionment of funds, there is no reason why a local community in a city should not control its police and certain other social services with the same authority a suburban or rural community enjoys. These are matters that make a difference in peoples' lives; they are key reasons why so many people, and not only the ghetto poor, believe themselves victimized, effectively disenfranchised. They are factors in the decay of politics in the liberal states.

V I I

There is a final matter which must be discussed when we ask why liberal government today is so resistant to reform, so stubborn in its perpetuation of incompetence. The characteristic sin of government bureaucracies is to assume that authority is justified by the fact that it exists. From Dickens' Circumlocution Office to Kafka's nightmare bureaucracies to the computerized administrations of the present day, the agency of government tends to validate itself by reference to itself. It looks on the public as material which needs to be processed. This is an inveterate problem.

The government's high civil servants can also easily come to believe that they serve a national interest which is distinct from the active public opinion of the moment. Particularly when they are under criticism and the public is in controversy, they can easily convince themselves that they are guardians of a permanent public interest above the passions of the moment. They can come to regard themselves, like the old French army, as grand but silent custodians of the nation, contemptuous of its passing controversies. Something like this has happened in recent years in America. Having "read the cables," possessing the secret knowledge — the reports and studies — generated within their own circles, officials have come to conceive of themselves as "tough-minded" guardians of the national interest. Those who criticize them, presumptively "tender-minded," simply do not share their knowledge or their responsibilities; the official comes to believe that "amateur" criticisms deserve to be disregarded, so far as that is possible.

This development is no novelty in the practice of government, but in its present American form mainly originated in matters of foreign policy. It still is most apparent in the State, intelligence and Defense agencies. It began a generation ago with the admirable effort by a small group of men professionally concerned with international politics to win the public over to an internationalist view of America's world role. Pearl Harbor settled that argument, but then the struggle began to convince the American public that the United States should play an active international role in the postwar world. High officials of the State and War departments allied themselves with the appointed officials of the Roosevelt and Truman Administrations to convince the country that there should be a bipartisan foreign policy of international responsibility and support for international organizations. The Republican party, led by Senator Arthur Vandenberg, was converted from its old isolationism. (The conversion was symbolized in the rejection, by the Republicans, of Senator Robert A. Taft as their presidential candidate in 1948 and again in 1952. This was a Republican concession not to principle — their hearts were with Taft — but to expediency: the American voter was in fact committed to internationalism.) Then came the mobilization of American public opinion to Cold War, foreign aid (the Marshall Plan and Point IV), and to a series of alliance commitments.

In Europe, during the same period, there were equivalent official, and officially inspired, campaigns to win and sustain public support for NATO, for high levels of armament, and the rearmament of Germany, for the series of steps which brought about European economic integration. Each of these efforts to shape public opinion — to win a public mandate — originated in a governmental or "establishment" elite and each was a success. And, in fact, each was an example of intelligent and competent political leadership: the leaders were doing what they were meant to do. They conceived relevant and intelligent programs, took them to the public, and won a *general mandate*. The common sense of the public found confirmation in these programs. The opposition to them remained within customary limits (except in France and Italy, where opposition was large but also dominated by the Communist parties which opposed liberal government itself and were thus regarded as self-excluded from the public consensus). In all of these cases, public approval was wide and effective. The people not only agreed to the policies but made sacrifices for them: in taxes for foreign aid and for arms, in peacetime military service.

But there have been other cases since the last war when "establishment" and popular beliefs came into clear conflict: in France and Britain at the time of the Suez campaign, in France as the Indochina and Algerian wars wore on, in the United States since the Vietnamese intervention in 1965. In each of these cases, while a segment of public opinion obviously supported the government, there was a lack of clear public mandate for what was being done. The ensuing official campaign to develop the mandate was unsuccessful: a majority, or vital minority, of the public remained hostile. The campaign then became a campaign not to convince the majority but to discredit the minority.

An often inarticulate or confused but stubborn opposition signified that the *common sense* of the public was affronted. The common sense of the public was that French and British colonial power could not be reimposed in the Middle East, that control of Indochina and Algeria was not worth the sacrifice to France and that the alternative solution of "association" no longer was viable. The common sense of the American public has been that war against a revolutionary guerrilla movement in an alien Asian society is unwise: and this has been as true for hawks as for doves — the former typically criticize the decision to intervene but conclude that what was a bad job to begin with must be ended with a victory, and ordinarily they have a very simple notion of what a victory would entail.

In each of these cases the Western government establishments, possessed by their own sense of priorities, committed by the political and moral investments already made, found themselves unable to *lead* the public. In default they chose to mislead and manipulate public opinion. A series of parliamentary or congressional evasions and expedients followed, deceptive official propaganda, outright lies, and efforts to ostracize or discredit the opposition. The results were inevitable: political crises in these countries, moral crises, and the fall of the governments concerned. In America the collapse of the Johnson Administration in 1968 was followed by Mr. Nixon's recovery of a national mandate by means of a program for Vietnam withdrawals. He recaptured the opposition's loyalty: that is to say, an acquiescence in his program which was contingent upon the program's success. In each case where its success, or Mr. Nixon's own good faith, subsequently came into doubt — as in Cambodia and Laos in 1970–1971 — the mandate was weakened. Since the Nixon program for Vietnam contains apparent contradictions and is unlikely to succeed, one must believe that he too faces an eventual and decisive breakdown of his mandate. The process of attack upon the opposition to isolate and discredit them has already begun, as the Nixon Administration intuitively prepares for the crisis.*

What these governments failed to understand in these cases is that the public trust — the public concession of legitimacy to a given government — is fairly fragile in a democracy and must be extensive, incorporating the vast majority of citizens on at least contingent and provisional terms — terms of "loyal opposition." This does not mean that government can only function to majority acclaim, or that government should turn itself to a supine subordination to public-opinion polls — which of course is a formula for no government at all. It does mean that government must grasp the difference between leadership — a matter of mobilizing and structuring public opinion to policy, serving the majority interest but maintaining the loyalty, the acquiescence and principled trust, of the opposition — and the tendency toward oligarchical or elite government. That tendency is toward suppressing the will, if not the persons, of the opposition (as "parasites," to quote Mr. Agnew, the Vice President of the United States,

---

* At the start of spring 1971, it is impossible to regard the future in Indochina without the darkest pessimism. The prospect is that "Vietnamization," conceived as allowing withdrawal of American ground troops while air power—and the threat of escalation—keep the Communists at bay, will effectively collapse. The Administration will then face these choices: American reassumption of the ground war with a halt to withdrawals—or new reinforcement; renewed bombing of North Vietnam, or an invasion of that country, or the threat or use of nuclear weapons, in an effort to force that decision which has eluded us for a decade; diplomatic settlement on the best terms obtainable, which will be bad ones for America; or a continued troop withdrawal which abandons the South Vietnamese to their fate. The final two possibilities, open to Mr. Nixon when he took office, now are vastly harder and more costly; they are also inconsistent with his course and commitments thus far in extending battle to Cambodia and Laos. Yet the military alternatives can hardly inspire confidence even in this Administration—although they are the more likely to be adopted. One must conclude that America—and battered Vietnam—will enter the 1972 election months in worse torment than in 1968.

speaking of war resisters and dissenters — parasites whom "we can afford to separate . . . from our society with no more regret than we should feel over discarding rotten apples from a barrel").

To determine what does and what does not constitute a popular mandate may be subtle or difficult when put in abstractions, but in practice it is perfectly clear — as Anthony Eden, Georges Bidault, Guy Mollet, Robert McNamara and Lyndon Johnson can attest. It derives from the neglected principle that what essentially characterizes and gives life to democratic government is regard for minorities, not simply that it obeys the will of the majority. There is little doubt that the Nazi government of Germany in the 1930's, or the Italian Fascist government of the same period, or the anti-Semitic dictatorships of Poland and Hungary before the war, or the paternalist Salazar regime in Portugal, or the present governments of Egypt and Indonesia and Cuba and North Vietnam, or indeed the Communist party's rule in Soviet Russia today, all more or less faithfully reflected a majority will in their countries — none of them, in a phrase of Stalin's, fit their peoples as a saddle fits a cow — but nobody has mistaken them for liberal democracies.

Democratic leadership requires a grasp of the fragile legitimacy which the public concedes, the need, in John C. Calhoun's words, for *concurrence* of the public, which is not the same thing as support or even agreement. No government in any but the most drastic crisis can expect to enjoy anything like unanimous public support. Its mandated function is, in any event, to propose action, to formulate problems and ways to deal with them, and this always is bound to be controversial. But when a government is unable to convince the greatest part of the public to grant at least provisional trust, to acknowledge the plausibility, the seriousness, of the government's course of action, then it has lost its mandate. Its position is bound to degenerate into public acrimony — if not actual acts of rebellion. The harmony of national government nearly always is polyphonic, even dissonant, but in this case it becomes cacophony. And then the political society itself, and not merely the government, is in jeopardy. That is what happened in the United States in the last years of the 1960's and persists today, and will grow worse. As Hannah Arendt has written, the dissenting minorities "are too important not merely in numbers but in *quality of opinion* to be safely disregarded."

In summary of the practical issues of liberal political reform, we are constrained in what we do by the fact that while the issues are profound, there is no single or sweeping solution for them. We are left with a series of partial remedies able to contribute to a restoration of competence in government, in turn contributing to a restoration of confidence and moral authority in the political society itself. But is this so extraordinary? The deeper issues of politics invariably are riddled with paradox and predicament, limited and contradictory possibilities. But only fools despair, as if this were some special curse of our own age.

CHAPTER VIII

Toward a Radicalism of Reason

Without slavery, as a matter of fact, there is no definitive solution. I very soon realized that. Once upon a time, I was always talking of freedom. At breakfast I used to spread it on my toast, I used to chew it all day long, and in company my breath was delightfully redolent of freedom. With that key word I would bludgeon whoever contradicted me; I made it serve my desires and power. I used to whisper it in bed in the ear of my sleeping mates and it helped me to drop them. I would slip it . . . Tchk! Tchk! I am getting excited and losing all sense of proportion. After all, I did on occasion make a more disinterested use of freedom and even — just imagine my naïveté — defended it two or three times without of course going so far as to die for it, but nevertheless taking a few risks. I must be forgiven such rash acts; I didn't know what I was doing. I didn't know that freedom is not a reward or decoration that is celebrated with champagne. Nor yet a gift, a box of dainties designed to make you lick your chops. Oh, no! It's a chore, on the contrary, and a long-distance race, quite solitary and very exhausting. No champagne, no friends raising their glasses as they look at you affectionately. Alone in a forbidding room, alone in the prisoner's box before the judges, and alone to decide in face of oneself or in the face of others' judgement. At the end of all freedom is a court sentence; that's why freedom is too heavy to bear, especially when you're down with a fever, or are distressed, or love nobody.

— The Narrator
in Albert Camus,
The Fall

I

THE CRISIS of liberalism comes out of the fact that we are condemned to freedom. The full meaning of this fate is only now being felt by modern society. The behavioral consequences are most marked in politics, the arena of public action, but the anxieties caused by freedom exist at all levels of life. This is why our contemporary political remedies either tend toward redemptive fantasy and eschatology — toward the redemptive transformation of all life, the achievement of a new sensibility among men — or they seem hopelessly inadequate. The achievement of a new sensibility or a new consciousness — those sentimental alternatives to real revolution — purports to be methods for accomplishing political and social change. But they are not methods at all, but evasions.

A new human consciousness, whether it is described in the language of revolution, counter-culture or sentimental liberalism, is not a method for causing political change but that transcendent condition which its advocates want to bring into existence through some unimaginable act of politics. If only some political program, some reorganization of society, could make humans feel free, feel satisfied, secure, fulfilled! Yet this would not be freedom; what these words describe is a condition of human security in which choices no longer have to be made and individual isolation has been replaced by solidarity, the desolation of existence in a universe of infinite choice no longer our common fate. What is sought is not freedom, as freedom actually exists in history and human society, but a release from terrible freedom.

The most profoundly felt loss in liberal society today is the loss of moral coherence, which is a loss of solidarity. The moral center is disintegrating, causing a series of incoherences and extravagances in our social and political behavior. Or to put it another way, modern society's confidence in its moral identity is being lost, and the reaction may be described by analogy to schizophrenia, with comparable manifestations of a divided self, of withdrawal and the indulgence of fantasy, of conduct intended to give reality to fantasies; or even catatonic behavior.

Or the matter is called a loss of values, which simply means that a great many people no longer accept the moral unities which were professed in the West until a few years ago, even though these people often are uneasy in their new agnosticism. Those who still believe are at the same time turned to an intensified reiteration and reaffirmation of belief in order to overcome doubt, not least their own doubt.

The things in which Western men once believed were monotheistic religion and science, or science in substitution for monotheism; in progress and human betterment as the outcome of scientific, reasoned organization and reform; in the efficacy of free debate and pragmatic action carried out according to a code of restraint. They affirmed a belief in human worth which owed its historical force to Western religion. They relied, inarticulately, upon a certain stability of institutions — institutions which assured them of their identity and provided a structure of meaning in their lives. They believed in a series of pieties concerning the nation — particular national traditions and national accomplishments.

While these beliefs nearly all have been shaken, the national community itself as a nexus of identity and human solidarity has not been weakened. The nationalist impulse is, if anything, more strongly felt than before because it supplies an identity which is, for many people in the modern West, the only important communal identification they still possess. With the intermediate associations of national and moral life broken down by the forces and velocity of contemporary change — class, craft, professional, religious communities — the nation remains; nationalism is reinforced. Moreover, the civil community fears anarchy. Primordial impulses of survival and security are here at work.

These "national" loyalties at the same time are today often displaced from the traditional nation. There is a particularist trend: a movement of loyalties away from the state toward racial and regional communities: black and American Indian "nationalisms," Québecois, Welsh, Scottish, Fleming, Breton, Tyrolean nationalisms. In these cases men alienated from the modern liberal state transfer their loyalties, their search for identity, to the surviving biological, linguistic and historical communities in modern society.

There is also, in Europe, some transfer of loyalty and self-identification to an entity larger than the nation, to Europe as a cultural community and a potential political agent. This has come as European political civilization's primacy in the world vanished; it is in part an affirmation of the unities of European culture against powerful external forces — European unities which today are understood as more significant than intra-European differences. This is a rational redirection of a community's political expectations as well as loyalties to a unit of society better able to act (in certain ways) in contemporary conditions. It is a practical political and social adaptation which does not have to usurp particular national traditions and linguistic cultures.

But practical as this adaptation may be, the "European" trend is also an affirmation of identity. It is not internationalist, or antinationalist, except in the narrowest sense. It is a new declaration of communal identity, directed to the community which assumes the greater modern relevance and importance. Here, as in the "nationalisms" of race and language, there is a significant emotional and nonrational content. The affirmation is particularist, "we" against "them."

I I

This new weight placed on national identification, inevitably political in its effect, poses a particular problem in America where nationalism has always been almost entirely political in content. As I suggested at the beginning of this book, the American cultural nation is hardly distinguishable from the political, constitutional, nation. Hence the peculiar intensity of the American reaction to national political incompetence and failure. European chauvinism, the Frenchman's conviction of French supremacy and even of a national *mission civilisatrice*, may be without specific political content, easily held by republican, monarchist, or anarchist. For the American it is bound up in a specific political structure and commitment, a political or ideological mission to the world (even when that mission, or meaning, may be defined in contradictory ways by individual Americans, as by a member of the Council on Foreign Relations on the one hand and a New Left militant on the other).

Thus the intensification of nationalist commitment as a response to lost community, to anomie, as a reaction against modern alienation, is peculiarly dangerous in America. It could bring about a new or reaffirmed American mission to — or against — the alien world. The new "European" consciousness of individual Europeans incorporates a more or less explicit recognition of this possibility. *Le défi américain,* the "American challenge," is political, even military, as well as economic and commercial. In today's international circumstances this American challenge (to Europe, and to the world) has come to involve a half-aware, half-contradictory, complicity with that other disoriented and challenged great power, the Soviet Union — a complicity which is rooted in shared frustration as well as shared primacy.

To the extent that the new nationalism amounts to a reaffirmation of community on a new scale, even with an increasingly political content, it can supply coherence and moral identity in remedy for the social dissolution of modern life. It commonly is spoken of in politics as a rightist tendency, but can as easily arise on the left — as already is the case in the Third World. This new nationalism will be a major component in the innovative politics of the years to come. It will be a lethal component if the new nationalism is translated to external mission in order to compensate for failures and moral disorders within the national community. The state, over the last half-century, has been burdened with expectations and responsibilities which go beyond politics, and our danger is that in the future the political order will increasingly be expected not only to give people security, civil order, a structure of economy, but to provide a transcendent purpose for individual life.

For this reason international politics and the foreign policies of nations provide a crucial area of attainable reform in our liberal crisis. The impulse to withdrawal, the avoidance of adventure, felt in Western Europe since 1945, has expressed a European intuition of the dangers in this situation. Europe's own very recent experience has been of devastation arising out of nationalisms which possessed a "total" relationship to anomic and crisis-ridden societies. Nazism, Fascism and Communism, all have been political movements which offered no mere civil order — making the trains run on time, or redistributing national wealth — but which attempted to give meaning and purpose to the lives of unhappy and drifting people.

In America the recent impulse to withdrawal from foreign interventions, the case made for "neo-isolationism," for a limited, pragmatic and unideological foreign policy, has expressed a fear of the kind of policies which express something like a total, totalitarian, relationship between the felt identity and sense of meaning in life of individual citizens and the international actions of their government. The crisis of liberal politics in American could dramatically be eased by a change in American policy toward the world; and in another way the crisis could be resolved on terrible terms if America were to continue to act out upon the world its own inner doubts and frustration. In either case what will be at work will be the American need to regain moral coherence and unity: even at grave cost.

I I I

American policy is interlocked with the national imperatives, needs and ideologies of others, and Russia, like America, is tempted to externalize its inner anguish and failure, to the world's pain. In this respect we are in conditions of world crisis, not simply a crisis of liberal politics. But to change America is possible (for Americans), and to do so can reduce the stress distorting the international system. A change in the foreign policies of the European states (or of Japan) could change things too, re-establishing international balance — as much a moral balance as a balance of power. The material resources to do this exist in Europe, even among the Common Market Six, and certainly they exist if Britain is added to the Six.

The argument can even be made that technologically advanced and socially homogeneous societies on the scale of the individual European nations, collaborating with one another in certain practical matters of collective security and economic and political action, in the foreseeable future will prove more vital political units than the United States or the Soviet Union. The latter, conglomerates of nationalities and races, today overextended in their foreign commitments and without clear means or designs for retrenchment or reform, ideologically exhausted, may actually be societies in decline. Their hypertrophic development of the old means of industrial war, total war, the weaponry which provides the chief manifestation of their strength today, may also prove a source of eventual paralysis. Their vast military establishments and armories may be a fatal overspecialization, in biological terms an adaptation to one specific threat (the threat of one another) which precludes adaptation to any other challenge. They may prove to be the modern social analogues of the invulnerably armored *Stegosaurus* — whose fate nonetheless proved to be the asphalt pit and the museum gallery. Russia and America already display their vulnerability to particularist nationalisms and racism, to political warfare, guerrilla warfare, subversion, and to the fateful sterility of attempting to repress internal divisions. They display signs of an inner disintegration which derives from their loss of political competence and moral coherence.

There will be, in a future not too distant from us today, a fundamental realignment of international power as a consequence of American and Soviet decline — or of their desperate efforts to prevent decline. Moreover, this realignment is likely to come on bad terms, for the question I asked earlier in this book — whether Europe and Japan have the will to act now in a creative way to change the international balance — must be given a provisionally negative answer. These states will only act under the destructive pressures of great-power decline and disorder. The European case for asserting a "Third Force" in world affairs, argued at the end of the 1940's, and the Gaullist program for an independent European world policy during the 1960's, both were premature. The first was clearly beyond postwar Europe's physical resources. The second was beyond contemporary Europe's psychological resources. Western Europe remains today too afraid of change, and at the same time too complacent, to be capable of great initiatives.

Eventually Europe will be compelled to act, but it now seems clear that there will be no calculated political settlement in Europe on Western initiative, able to alter the Soviet role in Eastern Europe and peacefully resolve

Russia's own unmanageable imperial inheritance. There will instead be a ragged and piecemeal breakup of the old Cold War arrangements, proceeding from American political isolation and troop withdrawals — from our turning inward, leaving Western Europe, and Germany, to make their own accommodations with an unstable Russia. The process has already begun; the West Europeans cling simultaneously to the remnants of NATO and a faith in detente. Eventually the West European nations probably will move closer to one another, with a shared strategic deterrent and development of an autonomous economy with a common currency, but this will be action taken under mounting external pressures and in conditions of political tension and economic conflict with America. Thus the American sense of isolation, of moral isolation, will be deepened.

Nor is an Asian settlement likely to come on any but bad terms for the self-esteem, to say nothing of the political interests, of the United States. A generation of localized instability in Asia was inevitable long before the American intervention on the mainland in the 1960's. Now a generation of international disorder there has been guaranteed, and the United States will be affected — and Japan. Japan is the great power of Asia, at the same time a zealot convert to the materialism of the industrial West: which is a more insecure faith than the Japanese as yet understand. Modern Japan too has its innocence to lose. The loss may have devastating consequences.

I V

The liberal crisis may be acted out in international politics; within the individual nations is where recovery is possible.

The nation is the political unit which our individual action can directly change and reform. It is crucial that we understand what it is that can be changed by political action. The fundamental struggle in politics in this century has been to keep it limited to the *polis*, the civic community, the civil order. The civil community relies upon the existence of a moral community, but the moral community can in turn be undermined by the incompetence, or the hubris and failure, of civil authorities. That is our present condition, and it is one for which the citizen of the liberal society must accept an individual responsibility. But the individual cannot expect too much from the civil authority.

It is inevitable that individuals want more from their civil community than competent administration of their common interests. They long to have purpose affirmed in their lives. They ask religious, philosophical, esthetic questions because in their contemporary condition of freedom they find themselves bereft of values and solidarity. Western man since the Enlightenment has carried out an immense and triumphant political and social enterprise, freeing the individual from the disablements of inherited class status, the ravages of institutionalized poverty, the value systems which validated the premodern social system of the West. This was done to liberate man; and we believed that man, thus liberated, could make a truly humane political order. We did not understand that freedom would also make men alone, isolated, faced with incalculable possibilities, masters of moral and material choices which would prove to be of terrifying importance. We did not understand that when the old closed world of absolutisms, divine authority, hierarchies, classes, churches was left behind, the new moral universe of liberty would be Promethean — and apocalyptic — in its possibilities.

In our own day the literary cult of the Marquis de Sade as existential figure, absolutely liberated man, expresses a contemporary grasp of the truth: that freed man of liberal society may consciously choose to try all possibilities, not merely those morally progressive adventures in co-operation and creativity which the sentimentalists had conceived. Why not discover the pleasures of cruelty, experiment with the ramifications of pain and death as much as with those of life? The modern sensibility ordinarily adds to its endorsement of all freedoms the injunction that others should not be hurt. But this is purely a reasonable limit; we must choose to observe it because we feel sympathy for others, or because we hold to a principle of the worth of others, or because we appreciate a need for reciprocity in society. Isolated man, technological man, the free man, can as rationally deny this; rationality in any event is the essential liberal virtue and the new man is in rebellion against the despised and failing liberal age of reason.*

The countervailing commitment can only be the act of an individual: a deliberate choice of reason, intelligence, and the moderation, reciprocity and pragmatism they enjoin, accepting that reason is fallible, full of contradiction, absurd. The alternative is to join the flight from reason

* The poet and critic George P. Elliott writes: ". . . once an unchristianed Westerner grants, as very many do, that value comes only from one's own nature, *sadisme* [as a philosophical principle] is very hard to crack. In the ferocity with which it pushes toward its extremest statement, it is the most disquieting possible travesty of liberal, progressive attitudes. *If there are no moral limits, why not?* To this argument decent liberals have no adequate reply, only sentiments. *I don't want to. I wish you didn't want to. You must be sick."*

which is actually a flight from the consequences, the condition, of freedom. In that case a man lives by intuition, fantasy, feeling and sensibility, but the political result is either withdrawal, one of the movements of private assertion; romantic nihilism, which often encompasses violence; or the quest for a millenarian solution.

V

The modern crisis arises from liberal culture, not merely liberal politics. What, then, is a political response worth? Is a political response even possible? The answer is yes because the political arena is where we can act. It is the only arena of valid public action. Our problem is not simply that we are modern industrial men, feeling the disintegrative impact of new social, economic and technological forces. As modern men in this condition we have also undergone a series of political follies and incompetences. War and stupidity have put us where we are today, and they can be remedied. The United States, certainly, has overreached itself and crashed into terrible contradictions for perfectly practical and identifiable reasons. The acts of the United States, then, have reverberated in the other liberal states for whom the American political success and the American role in international affairs have provided crucial points of orientation. The moral dependence of the other liberal states upon the United States has been very great since 1945. Those European states where liberal politics collapsed in the 1920's and 1930's still powerfully depend upon the United States to demonstrate that the liberal system can be an enduring success. Only in the countries where liberalism and republican government survived the last fifty years through native effort — even after degradation and recovery — is there an ability to be detached about the American ordeal: in France, England, Scandinavia. Even there it is not complete. The American role as paradigm of liberalism — *"Amerika, Du hast's besser,"* as Goethe put it — endures in the European imagination.

What is required, and constitutes the immense and honorable responsibility of political men, is radically intelligent and courageous reform of liberal politics — reform which at the same time accepts the limits and uncertainty of what public action can accomplish. We might call this a radical liberalism, or a rational radicalism — or an existential radicalism. What the words mean is clear enough, and undeniably hard to carry out.

We need first to clear away those social and economic problems of society which everyone knows how to solve — the clear failures and abuses and lapses in social services, law and the administration of justice, housing, medical treatment, environmental pollution and transport. This requires strong party and executive leadership able to make choices, to make a public case that can sustain a political mandate powerful enough to override established special interests, bureaucratic apathy and established forces of corruption. This category of obvious reforms includes, for Americans, ending the Vietnam war and retrenching and redisciplining our military, intelligence and diplomatic services to bring them into proportion with the real needs and interests of a nation no longer engaged in an intoxicating mission of world reform. But this much is also the easiest part of what we need.

The harder reform will come when we have turned the furious energies of our technocratic and political intelligentsia, of our academic men and social analysts, to a serious reconsideration of the right structure of liberal government and economy. We need to know a great deal more than we do now about how civil society can be made to function with close and effective links to the individual citizen, about the real possibilities of a great new devolution of political power, about how to discriminate between the necessities and economies of centralized power and the higher values of humane and accessible civil and social administration. We will need experiments as well as great debates. We need a big and intellectually exciting reform enterprise; we do not have it now — nor much evidence that it will come.

We need to give ordinary men a renewed *connection* with the political action of their society. Whether they customarily make use of that connection or not, it should exist, so that when the occasions arise which touch and move ordinary people, awakening them from indifference or preoccupation, they can make their will felt. Most people will inevitably ignore politics except when its crises or calamities are thrust upon them: what is crucial is that connection exists, and that they possess the knowledge that they can act and be heard. What is crucial is that the values of the governing elites remain democratic, which is to say that they remain constantly attentive to the fact that they are custodians of the easily shattered compact the people have made with one another — an agreement to live at peace with one another. Much is asked of these elites, intellectually and morally. A true radicalism for them is that they be honest with people, so that a public consensus can exist — *mimesis*, an ultimate and mutual respect between government and people, which comes from honesty in what is said and done.

To reconstruct the mechanisms and structures of politics, restoring competence in basic institutions of civil and economic administration, re-creating responsiveness and accessibility to popular feeling in government, will accomplish little directly to resolve the crisis of values. It merely is all that we can — as a practical matter — expect to do. Reform in liberal politics can relax some of the critical stresses in our society. It then becomes possible to imagine some reordering of our individual intellectual and moral accommodations to the deeper elements of disintegration in the modern West.

But it is the convention of books of social and political criticism to end with an affirmation of confidence in man's ability to master change and carry out reform — even when the simultaneous popular perception, as John Lukacs has remarked, is that the end of the world is in sight. The conventional optimism and the teleological expectation both are irrelevant to what has been said here — not because optimism is wholly absurd or because the end of the world may not be close, but because neither of these involve a course of action. The hardest of things to accept is that radical action to reform our society is necessary, and at the same time that political action is indeterminate in its consequences, paradoxical in effect.

To say this, I suppose, is to make a contra-liberal argument, since it contradicts the optimism which historically has been a vital component in liberal political culture. It is simply an argument of reason, evidenced by history — and reason is the other and more fundamental liberal commitment. We are free to do as we please; but to think and act to shape our society and make our political fate is appropriate to a Western liberal man.

We are also free to flee from our freedom, and the truth is that for a great many people today freedom is too much to bear. They take refuge in sentiment and sensibility, or in fantasy. Their flight from reason is made in the name of reason because they are blighted optimists: they wanted to believe that to be free is to be at rest, happy — the pursuit of happiness finished. But the reality of freedom, this liberation of man we have sought in the West since the eighteenth century, has proved to be an individual confrontation with the abyss of existence, where men are armed against desolation only by their power of affection and their reason. We turn from such starkness. Today, like birds striking against a glass, we beat against the meaning of freedom.

SOURCE NOTES

This is a political essay and not a work of research; accordingly, in what follows, I simply provide the sources for the quotations I have used and for certain statements into which some readers might wish to inquire more fully. The editions mentioned are those actually used.

CHAPTER I: The Crisis of Liberalism

Eric Partridge, *Origins: A Short Etymological Dictionary of Modern English*, 2d ed. (New York, Macmillan, 1959).

Glenn Tinder, *The Crisis of Political Imagination* (New York, Scribner, 1964), pp. 25-26.

T. S. Eliot, "Gerontion," in *Selected Poems* (Harmondsworth, Middlesex, Penguin Books, 1948).

Herbert Marcuse: his discussion of technology and political repression appears in *One-Dimensional Man* (Boston, Beacon Press, 1964); but see also his contributions to *A Critique of Pure Tolerance*, Essays by Robert Paul Wolff, Barrington Moore, Jr., and Herbert Marcuse (Boston, Beacon Press, 1966).

My Lai and today's generation of the young: this comment was first made in conversation by Edmund Stillman and seemed to me worth preserving. I appropriate it here with his good-natured consent.

Thomas Jefferson, letter of March 21, 1801, as quoted in Daniel J. Boorstin, *America and the Image of Europe* (New York, Meridian Books, 1960), p. 19.

Abraham Lincoln (in 1864), quoted in Shelby Foote, *The Civil War: A Narrative*, Vol. II, *Fredericksburg to Meridian* (New York, Random House, 1963), p. 948.

CHAPTER II: Social Dissolution

Gabriel Marcel, *The Decline of Wisdom* (London, The Harvill Press, 1954), p. 49.

Ivan Illich: both quotations are from an article entitled "Why We Must Abolish Schooling," *New York Review of Books* (July 2, 1970).

Anthony West, *Heritage* (New York, Pocket Books, 1957), pp. 176-177.

Torcuato S. Di Tella in a review article on populism in *Government and Opposition* (London, Autumn 1969).

On the Nazi party and German universities, see, *inter alia,* an article on the Weimar Republic by Walter Laqueur in the *New York Times Magazine* (August 16, 1970). On middle-class and professional membership in the Italian and Hungarian Fascist parties, see Herman Finer, *Mussolini's Italy* (New York, Universal Library, 1965), pp. 364 ff.; and István Deák in Hans Rogger and Eugen Weber, eds., *The European Right: A Historical Profile* (Berkeley and Los Angeles, University of California Press, 1965), pp. 396-397.

George L. Mosse, *The Crisis of German Ideology: Intellectual Origins of the Third Reich* (New York, Universal Library, 1964), p. 312.

The U.S. Labor Department report on blue-collar workers which I mention had not been formally released at this writing, but its substance was made known to the press and reported in several places, including *Time* magazine (July 13, 1970).

The remark by Freud is to be found in his *Civilization and Its Discontents* (London, 1930), p. 34, Note 1.

Norman Cohn, *The Pursuit of the Millennium: Revolutionary Messianism in Medieval and Reformation Europe and Its Bearing on Modern Totalitarian Movements* (New York, Harper Torchbooks, 1961), pp. 314-315, 319.

Jacques Ellul, *The Technological Society* (New York, Knopf, 1967), pp. 51-52.

Alessandro Pizzarno, "The Individualistic Mobilization of Europe," in Stephen R. Graubard, ed., *A New Europe?* (Boston, Houghton Mifflin, 1964), pp. 277-283. My data on worker migration in Europe, cited earlier, is drawn from Pizzarno and from standard UN sources. The figures on American worker mobility are from census data, including preliminary information made public on the 1970 census.

Irving Kristol, "Urban Civilization & Its Discontents," *Commentary* (July 1970).

Jo Grimond, "Bureaucratic Crush," *Commonweal* (September 20, 1968).

Charles Baudelaire, *Intimate Journals* (Boston, Beacon Press, 1957).

George Steiner, *The Death of Tragedy* (New York, Hill & Wang, 1963), p. 127.

Leszek Kolakowski, *The Alienation of Reason* (Garden City, N.Y., Doubleday, 1968).

CHAPTER III: The Burst Structures of Liberal Society

Eric Heller, quoted in W. H. Auden, *A Certain World: A Commonplace Book* (New York, Viking Press, 1970), p. 332.

Guglielmo Ferrero, *The Gamble: Bonaparte in Italy 1796-1797* (New York, Walker, 1961), pp. 297-298.

Russia as war-state: my remarks on this subject are based chiefly on my collaborator's contributions to Edmund Stillman's and my own *The Politics of Hysteria: The Sources of Twentieth Century Conflict* (New York, Harper, 1964), Chapter 7.

The British Secret Intelligence Service: Bruce Page, David Leitch and Phillip Knightley, *The Philby Conspiracy* (New York, New American Library, 1969), pp. 121-122.

European agricultural laborers before 1914: see especially Ronald Blythe, *Akenfield: Portrait of an English Village* (New York, Pantheon, 1969).

Rexford Tugwell: from his diary, quoted in William Leuchtenberg, *Franklin D. Roosevelt and the New Deal, 1932-1940* (New York, Harper, 1963), p. 19. The quotation from Elmer Davis is in Leuchtenberg, pp. 26-27.

Michael Novak, "Politicizing the Lower-Middle," *Commonweal* (June 6, 1969).

Poujadism: the quotations are taken from Sean E. Fitzgerald, "The Anti-Modern Rhetoric of Le Mouvement Poujade," *The Review of Politics* (April 1970).

Worker attitudes on Vietnam: see especially Harlan Hahn, "Dove Sentiments Among Blue-Collar Workers," *Dissent* (May–June 1970).

Stewart Alsop, column in *Newsweek* (June 29, 1970).

CHAPTER IV: The International Crisis

F. Scott Fitzgerald, *The Crack-Up*, Edmund Wilson, ed. (New York, New Directions, 1945), p. 208.

George Steiner, *op. cit.*

Gabriel Kolko, *The Politics of War* (New York, Random House, 1968) and *The Roots of American Foreign Policy: An Analysis of Power and Purpose* (Boston, Beacon Press, 1969).

Noam Chomsky, *American Power and the New Mandarins* (New York, Pantheon, 1969).

Dean Rusk, "Guidelines of U.S. Foreign Policy," *The Department of State Bulletin* (Washington, June 28, 1965), p. 1033.

Edmund Stillman and William Pfaff, *The New Politics: America and the End of the Postwar World* (New York, Coward-McCann, 1961), p. 173.

CHAPTER V: The Failure of the Left

Adolf Hitler, quoted in Hermann Rauschning, *Hitler Speaks* (London, Eyre & Spottiswoode, 1939).

George Lichtheim, *The Concept of Ideology and Other Essays* (New York, Random House, 1967), p. 264.

The left as a political success in the West: for thoughtful statements of the case against this argument of mine, see columns by Tom Kahn in *New America* (November 24, 1969, and February 25, 1970), and a letter from Gus Tyler in *Commentary* (February 1970), both responding to my article "The Decline of Liberal Politics" in *Commentary* (October 1969).

Lenin, *The State and Revolution* (London, Allen & Unwin, 1917).

The Webbs: the lines quoted appear in Anne Fremantle, *This Little Band of Prophets: The British Fabians* (New York, New American Library, 1959), p. 112. The remark by Sydney Olivier is quoted on p. 89.

Nathan Glazer, "The New Left and Its Limits," *Commentary* (July 1968).

Michael Harrington, "Why We Need Socialism in America," *Dissent* (May-June 1970).

On a "conscience constituency" as the basis for a new American party of the left, see especially Michael Harrington, *Toward a Democratic Left* (New York, Macmillan, 1968), Chapter 10.

Max Beloff, "Universities and Violence," *Survey* (London, October 1968).

Lewis S. Feuer, *Conflict of Generations* (New York, Basic Books, 1969).

Theodore Roszak, *The Making of a Counter-Culture* (New York, Anchor, 1969). The statement that we have "turned from objective consciousness . . ." is on p. 215. On a "shamanistic" world view, see especially Chapters 7 and 8.

Paul Goodman, "The New Reformation," *New York Times Magazine* (September 14, 1969). This article is also included in his book *New Reformation* (New York, Random House, 1970).

R. D. Laing: his influence upon the New Left and the development of the new sensibility has chiefly been through his *Politics of Experience* (New York, Pantheon, 1967) in which he says: "We are potentially men, but are in an alienated state, and this state is not simply a natural system. . . . [We are] mad, even, from an ideal standpoint we can glimpse but not adopt" (p. 13). In his challenge to the conventional definitions of madness, Laing develops an argument originally made in historical terms by Michel Foucault in *Madness and Civilization: A History of Insanity in the Age of Reason* (New York, Pantheon, 1965). Both books possess an interest and importance beyond that of most that has been written about and from within the New Left.

Rudi Dutschke, quoted in Philip Shabecoff, "The Followers of Red Rudi," *New York Times Magazine* (April 28, 1968).

Goodman, *loc. cit.*

Maurice Cranston, "Herbert Marcuse," *Encounter* (London, March 1969). On Marcuse's own views, in addition to the books cited above, see his *Soviet Marxism: A Critical Analysis* (London, Routledge & Kegan Paul, 1958); and *Reason and Revolution: Hegel and the Rise of Social Theory* (New York, Oxford, 1941). His argument about "non-repressive" culture appears in *Eros and Civilization* (Boston, Beacon Press, 1955).

Susan Sontag: her writings on Vietnam in *Styles of Radical Will* (New York, Farrar, Straus & Giroux, 1969).

Christopher Lasch, *The Agony of the American Left* (New York, Vintage, 1969); see especially Chapter 2.

Max Beloff, *op. cit.*

Yves Simon, *Community of the Free* (New York, Holt, 1947), p. x.

CHAPTER VI: The Future of Ideology

Albert Camus, *Resistance, Rebellion, and Death* (New York, Knopf, 1961), p. 121.

Alexis de Tocqueville, *Democracy in America*, Vol. II (New York, Vintage, 1954), pp. 336-337. The second quotation from Tocqueville is from *The European Revolution and Correspondence with Gobineau*, ed. and transl. by John Lukacs (New York, Anchor, 1959), p. 165.

Jacob Burckhardt, *Judgements on History and Historians* (Boston, Beacon Press, 1958), pp. 218-220.

Louis-Ferdinand Céline, *Journey to the End of the Night*, transl. by John H. P. Marks (New York, New Directions, 1960), p. 9.

Karl Jaspers, *Man in the Modern Age* (New York, Anchor, 1957), p. 3.

Bede Griffiths, O.S.B., *The Golden String* (New York, Kenedy, 1955), p. 39.

Georges Bernanos, *The Last Essays of Georges Bernanos* (Chicago, Regnery, 1955), pp. 94-95.

John Lukacs, *Historical Consciousness, or The Remembered Past* (New York, Harper, 1968), pp. 307-308.

Giuseppe di Lampedusa, *The Leopard*, transl. by Archibald Colquhoun (New York, Pantheon, 1960), p. 287.

Benjamin Disraeli, *Coningsby* (New York, New American Library, 1962), Chapter 5.

Robert Jay Lifton, *History and Human Survival: Essays on the Young and Old, Survivors and the Dead, Peace and War, and on Contemporary Psychohistory* (New York, Random House, 1970), p. 276.

Hugh Seton-Watson, *Neither Peace nor War: The Struggle for Power in the Postwar World* (New York, Praeger, 1960); see especially Chapter 7.

Daniel Berrigan, "Looking at Catonsville," *Worldview* (May 1970).

Heinrich Himmler: the quotation is taken from Roger Manvell and Heinrich Fraenkel, *Himmler* (New York, Paperback Library, 1968), p. 147.

Hans J. Morgenthau, *Politics in the Twentieth Century*, Vol. III, *The Restoration of American Politics*, "The Revival of Objective Standards" (Chicago, The University of Chicago Press, 1963).

CHAPTER VII: The Problem of Liberal Reform

J. L. Talmon, "Sorel's Legacy," *Encounter* (London, February 1970).

Daniel Bell, quoted in Arendt, below, *loc. cit.*

Hannah Arendt, *On Violence* (New York, Harcourt, Brace, 1970), pp. 100-101.

Zbigniew Brzezinski, "America in the Technotronic Age," *Encounter* (London, January 1968).

John Kenneth Galbraith: he has stated the "zero growth" argument in an article in the *Asahi Evening News* (Tokyo), quoted in *The Times* (London, September 2, 1970).

Tom Wicker, column in the *New York Times* (August 9, 1970).

General de Gaulle's proposal for a reconstructed "Charlemagne empire"; from a speech delivered on March 16, 1950, quoted in Alexander Werth, *De Gaulle* (New York, Simon and Schuster, 1966), pp. 216-217.

John Mander, "The Future of Social Democracy," *Commentary* (September 1970).

Peter F. Drucker, *The Age of Discontinuity: Guidelines to Our Changing Society* (New York, Harper, 1969).

Theodore J. Lowi, *The End of Liberalism: Ideology, Policy, and the Crisis of Public Authority* (New York, Norton, 1969). The quotation is from p. 233.

Richard Goodwin: see his article "The Sources of Public Unhappiness" in *The New Yorker* (January 4, 1969), in which he argues for transferring government power to "the smallest unit consistent with the scale of the problem," in fact a basic principle of the prewar Catholic Distributist movement.

Arthur Schlesinger, Jr., *The Crisis of Confidence* (Boston, Houghton Mifflin, 1969).

Thomas Jefferson: I have taken this quotation from an (undated) broadside issued by Citizens for Local Democracy (111 Mercer Street, New York 10012), an organization promoting local political control.

Spiro Agnew, quoted by Hannah Arendt in an article on civil disobedience in *The New Yorker* (September 12, 1970).

Hannah Arendt, *ibid.*

CHAPTER VIII: Toward a Radicalism of Reason

Albert Camus, *The Fall*, transl. by Justin O'Brien (New York, Knopf, 1957), pp. 132-133.

George P. Elliott, "Never Nothing," *Harper's* (September 1970).

John Lukacs, *op. cit.*, p. 314.

INDEX

advertising of unnecessary goods, 52, 114
affluent society, 24–25, 30, 40, 54, 81, 104, 114, 150
Agnew, Spiro, 61, 110; quoted, 175–76
agrarian societies, 29, 31, 35, 45, 46, 135
Algerian war, French, 82, 120n, 160, 173
Alsop, Stewart, on the draft, 63
"American challenge," 185
"Americanization" of Europe, 150
American Revolution, 12
anarchism, 116, 119
anxieties, new, 6, 16, 19, 25, 60, 67, 98, 102, 104, 122, 134, 153, 154, 158, 159, 169, 181; based on conservative longings, 125–30
Arendt, Hannah, quoted, 148, 177
aristocracies, end of, 131
Asian policy, U.S., future of, 189
astrology and the New Left, 137

Baudelaire, Charles, quoted, 39
Bell, Daniel, 140, 148
Beloff, Max, 109–10; quoted, 120
Bernanos, Georges, 115; quoted, 129
Berrigan, Daniel, quoted, 138
black militants, 6, 56, 65, 72, 102, 108–9, 116, 117, 139
black nationalism, 183
blacks, see Negroes; Race problems
Bolshevism, 39, 47–48, 50, 55. See also Communism; Russia
Brandt, Willy, 104, 107
Breton, André, quoted, 119
British Broadcasting Corporation, 164
"Brown Bolshevism," 48
Brzezinski, Zbigniew, quoted, 149
Burckhardt, Jacob, 131; quoted, 126–27

bureaucratization, 46, 64, 96, 100, 129, 130, 149, 157, 164, 171
Byron, Lord George, quoted, 90

Calhoun, John, 176
Camus, Albert, quoted, 124, 180
capitalism, 19; and the liberal left, 95–96, 137; reform of, 163
Céline, Louis, quoted, 127
Central Intelligence Agency, 49, 172
Centralization of power, 34–36, 98, 114, 125–27, 148, 166–67
change, need for, 44, 92, 107, 142, 145–46, 162, 164, 167, 195
China, Communist, 28, 74, 77, 81, 84, 85, 117
Chomsky, Noam, 80n, 117
Christianity, 56, 57, 111n, 135
cities, problems of, 100, 102, 127, 152, 156, 170
class issues, in politics, 25
class mobility, 30, 32–34
Cohn, Norman, quoted, 27
cold war, 6, 49, 83–87, 172, 189
Comintern, 49–50
Common Market, European, 160, 187
Communism, 51, 84, 116, 173, 186; U.S. fear of, 74–76
Communist Manifesto, quoted, 27–28
confidence, political, loss of, 3, 5, 13–14, 38, 55–58, 64–65, 82; recovery of, 158
Congress, U.S., 60, 96, 163. See also Representative government
"conscience constituency," 104, 107
conservatives and conservatism, 3, 96, 131–34; Disraeli on, 132n, 133n; and the new anxieties, 125–30; and the New Left, 137; today's reactionaries, 135–36; weaknesses of, 140, 146

205

Index

economy, 52–53; public approval of, 172–77; streamlining of, 164. *See also* Confidence; Mandate; Responsiveness

governments, liberal, *see* Liberal governments; local, 165–66, 168; state (U.S.), 166; totalitarian, *see* Totalitarianism

Greece, 96, 135, 136

Griffiths, Bede, 131; quoted, 128

Grimond, Jo, quoted, 38

gross national product, 149–50

Guevara, Che, 120*n*, 138

Harrington, Michael, quoted, 104

Heller, Eric, quoted, 44

helplessness, *see* Powerlessness

Himmler, Heinrich, quoted, 139*n*, 140

Hitler, Adolf, 4, 71, 75, 139, 140; quoted, 90

Hungary, Soviet invasion of, 85*n*

identity, search for, 183–84

ideology, end of, 140

Illich, Ivan, quoted, 20

individual, in modern society, 29, 36, 58–59, 125–27; powerlessness of, *see* Powerlessness

Indochina war, French, 79, 82, 173

industrialization, 19–22, 36; industrial revolution, 28–29; Marx and Engels on, 27–28. *See also* Technology

industrial mortality in U.S., 31

Industrial Workers of the World, 116*n*

institutions, perfection of, 146–47

intellectual, duty of, 124

internationalism, liberal, 79, 172; missionary, 11*n*, 12, 79–81, 193

international politics, stage for moral action, 58, 187–89. *See also* Foreign policy

interventionism, 9, 12, 157*n*. *See also* Internationalism

isolationism, 9, 12, 81, 172, 186, 189

Italy, 6, 23, 176; today, 29, 30, 46, 112, 118, 155, 163, 168, 169*n*, 173

Jacobins, 121

Japan, 87, 187–89

Jaspers, Karl, quoted, 127–28

Jefferson, President Thomas, quoted, 11*n*, 168

Johnson, President Lyndon, and his Administration, 64, 79, 99, 140, 174, 176

justice, lack of, 154–56, 193

Kafka, Franz, 171

Kennedy, President John, and his Administration, 37–38, 79, 99

Kennedy, Robert, 65

knowledge, specialization of, 37

Know-Nothing movement, 133

Kolakowski, Leszek, quoted, 41

Kolko, Gabriel, 80*n*, 117

Kristol, Irving, quoted, 34, 35

labor unions, and the poor, 105; violence of, 55; *See also* Workingmen

Lacqueur, Walter, quoted, 139

Lampedusa, Giuseppe di, 131–32

Lasch, Christopher, quoted, 118

Latin America, 134

law and order, 154–56

Left, political, accomplishments of, 91, 95, 97–98, 103; and capitalism, 95–96; defined, 92; failure of, 91, 96–97, 102–5; history of, 92–94; programs of, 95, 118. *See also* New Left

LeMay, General Curtis, quoted, 139*n*

Lenin, Vladimir, 117; quoted, 99*n*

Leninism, 84, 118–21

liberal economy, history of, 51–55

liberal governments, accomplishments of, 145, 150, 190; breakdown of, 96–97, 102–3, and reason for, 147*n*; crisis of, 3–8, 56, 60–67; history of, 45, 47, 50–51; opponents of, 66; pre-liberal governments, 134. *See also* Confidence, loss of

liberalism, characterized, 56; crisis of, 3–16; defined, 2; and New Left, compared, 137–40; and

207

Index

politics, European, 50–51, 94, 103
politics, U.S., changes in, 34; and class issues, 25; crisis of, 3–8; and culture, 184, 190; and economic struggles, 25–26; importance of, 10–11; need for new, 142, 144, 145, 163; political parties, 94, realignment of, 103–9
pollution, industrial, 7, 9, 41, 155, 163, 193
poor, the, 19, 20, 32, 56, 97, 156, 170; unionization of, 105. See also Poverty programs
population growth, 9, 129n; migration, 30–31
Populism, 23n, 54, 119, 146, 161. See also New Populism
pornography, new, 73
Port Huron statement, 122
Portugal, 6, 30, 96, 134, 136n, 176
Poujadism, 4, 61
poverty programs, failure of, 100–1, 152, 164–65. See also the Poor
Powell, Enoch, 161
power, centralization of, 35–36, 125–27, 166–67
powerlessness of the individual, 53, 59–61, 64–65, 99, 102, 112, 127–28, 130, 153, 155, 194; of the poor, 20; remedy for, 169–70
production, Marx and Engels on, 27–28
propaganda, 47, 50
public opinion polls, 51, 62–63, 175
Puritanism, 72, 78, 79, 150; in the New Left, 115

race problems, in U.S., 6, 102, 108–9, 152, 168, 170
radicalism, as a political force, 145–146
reason, need for, 57, 128, 142, 191–93, 196
reform, failure of, 101; technocratic, 146–49, 151–54; 167; world, 11–12, 193. See also Change, need for; Missionary internationalism
regulatory agencies, 164

religion, and the counter-culture, 111n; and the New Left, 137; and politics, 50, 57; shakening of, 29, 41–42, 182
representative government, 51, 59; created, 45; failure of, 96
"repressive tolerance," 125–26
Republican morality, 35
Republican party, U.S., 62, 79, 94, 99, 133, 172
responsiveness, government, to the public, 15, 64, 65, 195. See also Mandate, public
revenue sharing, in U.S., 55, 169
revolution, Byron on, 90; Guevara on, 138
revolutionaries, in U.S., 6–7, 55, 66, 94, 106
Rhineland, German march into, 71
Roosevelt, President Franklin, 55, 172
rootlessness, 27, 35
Roszak, Theodore, quoted 110–11
Rusk, Dean, quoted, 80
Russia, under Communism, 28, 49, 81, 83, 95, 157n, 176, 185, 187, 188; history of, 84, 88; Revolution, 39, 47–48, 55, 110; U.S. relations with, see Cold war

Sade, Marquis de, 191
Salazar, Antonio de, 135, 136n, 176
science, as a threat, 8, 125, 128; and the New Left, 137. See also Technology
Secret Service, British, 49n
socialism and socialists, 54, 93, 94, 98, 99n, 116; goals and programs, 104, 107, 162–63; and the New Left, compared, 138
South, U.S., 114, 115, 132, 167, 168
Soviet Union, see Russia
Spain, 6, 30, 96, 117, 134, 136n, 161
Spanish Civil War, 116n
specialization of knowledge, 37
Stalin, Joseph, and Stalinists, 46, 54, 74, 83–85, 88, 176
"states' rights," 168
Steiner, George, 41; quoted, 70

ABOUT THE AUTHOR

William Pfaff was born in Iowa in 1928, and attended public and parochial schools there and in Columbus, Georgia. He was graduated from the University of Notre Dame in 1949.

His three earlier books are *The New Politics*, *The Politics of Hysteria*, and *Power and Impotence*, all collaborations with Edmund Stillman. He has also contributed essays to Irving Howe's *A Dissenter's Guide to Foreign Policy*, John Kirk's *America Now*, the Hudson Institute volume *Can We Win in Vietnam?*, and other books. He lectures, and writes frequently for the national press.

Mr. Pfaff became an editor of *Commonweal* in 1949, and in subsequent years was a correspondent in Europe, Africa, and Asia, and an executive of the Free Europe Committee. During and after the Korean War he served with infantry and Special Forces units. He joined Hudson Institute in 1961, later taking leave for a year's writing in France and Italy under a Rockefeller Foundation Grant in International Studies and as a Senior Fellow of the Columbia University Russian Institute.

Mr. Pfaff is married and has a son and daughter. He lives with his family in an eighteenth-century house in Ridgefield, Connecticut.